THEY COULDN'T HAVE DONE IT WITHOUT US

THEY COULDN'T HAVE DONE IT WITHOUT US

THE MERCHANT NAVY
IN THE FALKLANDS WAR

JOHN JOHNSON-ALLEN

SEAFARER BOOKS

First published in the UK by
Seafarer Books
102 Redwald Road
Rendlesham
Woodbridge
Suffolk IP12 2TE
www.seafarerbooks.com

ISBN 978-1-906266-23-3

A catalogue record for this book is available from the British Library

Edited by Hugh Brazier
Typesetting by Julie Rainford
Cover design by Louis Mackay
Drawings by Louis Roskell
Proofreading by Eric Cowell

Printed in Finland by Bookwell OY

For David Smith, who encouraged me

Contents

Foreword

Admiral Sir Michael Layard, KCB, CBE

I am immensely touched and honoured to be invited to write the foreword to this important and fascinating book that fills an obvious gap in the chronicles of the Falklands Conflict of 1982 – the crucial Merchant Navy story. I have a long and varied association with the merchant service which started when I was a pupil at the Nautical College, Pangbourne, in 1949, after which I joined the Royal Navy, while many of my chums left to become distinguished members of our sister service, the Merchant Navy. During my time in the Royal Navy I was, of course, a frequent and grateful customer of the great merchant-manned Royal Fleet Auxiliary, both as an aviator in aircraft carriers and as the commanding officer of various warships.

My main association with the Merchant Navy came during the Falklands campaign, when I was given the task of resurrecting the laid-up Cunard container ship *Atlantic Conveyor*, converting her to provide two flight decks and filling her with Harriers, helicopters and a myriad of stores, weapons and associated people, before setting off to join the Task Force in the exclusion zone off the Falkland Islands. You will read the story of our conversion, brief service and destruction in the pages of this book. Suffice to say, it was an extraordinary experience, made infinitely more so by my admiration and affection for the captain, Ian North, and his superb team of officers and men. My respect and regard for their adaptability, energy and courage knew no bounds and captured for me the essence of our great merchant service and its people, to which we all owe so much throughout its five-hundred-year history. But ours was a single story in the Falklands conflict, for over seventy merchant ships in various roles were involved – and, as the title so aptly suggests, We Couldn't Have Done It Without Them.

I commend this excellent and seminal book, which tells a riveting story in a clever mix of personal anecdote, document and comment.

Acknowledgements

Since I started on the research for this book, I have had an enormous amount of support, encouragement and help from a great many people and from some very unexpected sources. I have been welcomed into homes from Yorkshire to Hampshire and Northamptonshire to Norfolk. The common thread has been the enthusiasm of everyone with whom I have been in contact, corresponded with or met, to raise the profile of the Merchant Navy's involvement in the Falklands conflict.

My thanks go to the following, whose help was deeply appreciated:

Sukey Cameron (Falklands Islands Government Representative), Alison Harris, Gill Marriner, Dr Kathy Kestin, Lauraine Mulberry, Anne-Marie Scott-Masson

Admiral Sir Michael Layard

Vice-Admiral Sir Jeremy Blackham

Captains Jack Beaumont, Anthony Braithwaite, Jeremy Carew, Don Cockrill, David Ede, David Gerrard, John Hughes, Don Jarvis, Michael Lacey, Stuart Lawrence, Martin Reed, Richard Woodman

Steve Cockburn, Don Cole, Charles Drought, Andrew Flewker, Peter James, John Kelly, Malcolm Orr, Maurice Onslow, Louis Roskell, Graham Wallace.

All the photographs have come from private collections, and the vast majority were taken by the contributors. Louis Roskell also provided the wonderfully atmospheric artwork, including the front cover.

The accounts in this book were taken from contemporary diaries and recollections written immediately after the events, while others were written specifically for this book. Further information may become available from the National Archive in 2012, when the official files will be opened. I am responsible for the connecting text, and any errors that occur therein are mine alone.

Once again I have enjoyed enormous support from my publisher, Seafarer Books. Patricia, Hugh, Julie and Louis have worked their magic to produce what you have before you.

Last but definitely not least, I am grateful to my wife Claire, indefatigable proofreader and total support – even when I wasn't helping in the garden!

John Johnson-Allen
October 2011

Introduction

On 2 April 1982, Argentinian forces invaded the Falkland Islands, a British overseas territory in the South Atlantic. Two days later the Queen signed an Order in Council, taking the United Kingdom to war against Argentina.

That this particular war had broken out can be traced back to 1832, when the British government took and maintained possession of the Falkland Islands (there had been earlier occupations of the islands by other powers for brief periods). British possession was never accepted by Argentina, and by 1982 the internal politics of that country were such that an invasion to reclaim the Islas Malvinas, as they were known by Argentina, had been planned for some time. Initially, a diversionary action at South Georgia took place, involving civilian contractors who landed without permission in mid March. This put the British government on a heightened state of awareness, and the Argentinian invasion plan was therefore set in train at the end of March 1982. The Argentinian invasion of the Falklands took place on the morning of 2 April, and Governor Rex Hunt surrendered to the Argentinian forces, against the wishes of the locally based Royal Marine contingent, that same morning.

The naval operation to retake the islands, authorised by Prime Minister Margaret Thatcher against the advice of Defence Secretary John Nott, was christened Operation Corporate. Admiral Sir Henry Leach, the First Sea Lord at the time, set in train the assembly of a Naval Task Force, with enough support ships to take the necessary troops and equipment from the United Kingdom to the Falkland Islands. The South Georgia landing had given early indications of an impending crisis in the area, and two submarines had already left the United Kingdom for the South Atlantic, one on 31 March and the other on 1 April. The warships started to leave on 5 April – HMS *Hermes* and HMS *Invincible* were the first to leave. Within seven days after the Order in Council was signed, the first merchant ships to depart were the P&O liner *Canberra* and the P&O ferry *Elk*. The former was carrying 40 and 42 Royal Marine

Commando and 3 Para, while their equipment, stores and ammunition was on board the *Elk*. Other vessels departed in quick succession thereafter. The re-occupation of the Falklands by the main invasion force on the *Canberra*, together with 2 Para, who were on the North Sea ferry *Norland*, began on 21 May. Before that date there had been naval casualties on both sides. HM Submarine *Conqueror* sank the Argentinian heavy cruiser *General Belgrano* on 2 May,[1] and two days later HMS *Sheffield* was hit by an Exocet missile and subsequently sank.

The Argentinian army surrendered, after fierce fighting, on 14 June, and some of the Royal Navy and merchant ships returned to the UK soon afterwards. Other ships remained in the South Atlantic for several months, however, carrying out necessary functions for the British Army, which was still ashore.

The military and naval elements of the Falklands War have been thoroughly chronicled by many different writers, and over 70 books have been written on the subject. In addition, the contribution of the Royal Fleet Auxiliary has been described in detail by Geoff Puddefoot.[2] However, the Merchant Navy's activities are much less well known. Laurence Freedman, the official historian of the Falklands War, perhaps revealed something of the official attitude when he dismissed the Merchant Navy as 'an impenetrable mystery, girt about by seasickness'.[3] The aim of this book is to lift the curtain on that mystery and reveal the experiences of some of the men and women of those merchant ships who made the invasion possible.

Other accounts have been published – the part played by *QE2*, for example, has been written about by Carol Thatcher[4] and Commodore R Warwick,[5] amongst others,[6] as part of a wider story. But no book has yet been entirely dedicated to the part that the Merchant Navy played in the Falklands War, and

---

[1] A detailed account of this sinking has been written by Mike Rossiter, *Sink the Belgrano*, London, 2007.

[2] G Puddefoot, *No Sea too Rough*. London, 2007.

[3] L Freedman, The Official History of the Falklands Campaign, 2 vols. London, 2005.

[4] C Thatcher,*QE2: 40 Years Famous*. London, 2007.

[5] RW Warwick, QE2: the Cunard Line Flagship Queen Elizabeth 2. London, 1999.

[6] See, for example, P Rentell, *Master Mariner*. Rendlesham, 2009.

in particular there has been very little research into the activities of the personnel who crewed the ships.

Finding the contributors for this book, for the events of nearly 30 years before, involved asking many people where they had been in April 1982, and if they hadn't been there themselves, if they knew anybody who had. In addition, questions left on online maritime forums also produced some valuable replies. The generosity of seafarers in lending their personal diaries of those days has been remarkable. My research also involved going to meet people, who searched through their lofts to find photographs, documents and diaries, and then searched through their memories to remember what had happened and dictated it to the voice recorder.

The accounts that are written are, for the most part, personal accounts, either taken from contemporary diaries or written especially for this book. In some instances quotations from other publications are used, because this was the most effective way to depict the activities of a particular ship. The spread of activities of the writers of the accounts is as wide as could be found, ranging from a second cook/baker to several ships' masters, by way of an assortment of navigating officers, radio officers, engineer officers and electrical officers.

The images of the Falklands Conflict recalled by the majority of people are those of the Royal Marines 'yomping' across open country, or the *Sheffield* or *Sir Galahad* on fire, or paras with camouflaged faces. But very few people stop to think how 8000 troops arrived there – although some may have memories of the *Canberra* or the *QE2*, which were iconic ships in their own right. Seeing the familiar, military, aspects of the Falklands War, almost nobody gives any thought to how the troops' equipment, food, stores and fuel, which kept the war going, arrived there. The Falkland Islands are 8000 miles away from Britain, and the only way to transport supplies there was by sea. To keep the military machine supplied, over 70 ships were needed. Merchant ships. And all the personnel on those merchant ships were volunteers, who had had the chance to decline to go. One senior marine superintendent, with his seagoing days long behind him, seeing one of his company ships off, was asked by his wife, 'Would you have liked to be on board?' He replied, 'I would have sailed as cabin boy.' That ship was the *Atlantic Conveyor*.

In April 1982 the British Merchant Navy was called upon to do once more what it has done for five centuries: with its ships and its men it supported the Royal Navy in time of war. However, by 1982 the Merchant Navy was much diminished from what it had been for most of the twentieth century, when the Red Ensign was seen throughout the world and merchant ships, in two world wars, had prevented the country from coming to its knees through lack of supplies. After the Second World War the fleet was rebuilt, and by 1960 it had regained, in tonnage terms, its pre-war position. But because of the growth of other fleets, such as the Norwegian and the Liberian, the British merchant fleet's share of the world total of shipping had slipped to just 16 per cent – in 1900 it had been 45 per cent. The situation was not helped by British shipbuilding output: in 1948 it accounted for 57 per cent of world output, but by 1966 it had shrunk to a mere 7 per cent. The huge growth in tanker fleets in the 1960s had come to an end and, because of the oversupply of ships, by the 1970s some 47 million tons of tankers were laid up worldwide.

The change in world trading conditions also meant that redundancies among British Merchant Navy personnel were drastic in their extent. One major tanker company made its entire contracted seagoing staff redundant in a single day, advising them to apply to a manning agency to retain their jobs. There were also many company amalgamations and mergers, and the traditional companies that had been in existence for over a century were disappearing.

By the time of the Falklands conflict, the UK merchant fleet had declined to 29 million tons of shipping, from 50 million tons only seven years before – a loss of 40 per cent over that period. The numbers of British officers in the Merchant Navy had fallen from 41,000 in 1975 to 28,000 in 1982. And this decline has continued, as successive governments have avoided any sort of financial or fiscal assistance to the shipping industry. The total number of all seafarers at sea in 2008 in the British Merchant Navy was 14,600.

And yet, from this rapidly declining fleet, 52 merchant ships were taken up in 1982 to support the Royal Navy, in addition to 22 Royal Fleet Auxiliary ships and two Royal Maritime Auxiliary ships, all crewed by Merchant Navy personnel. Chapter 1 describes the range of ships involved and summarises the roles they played, before we turn to the personal accounts of the merchant seamen themselves, in Chapters 2 to 8.

Not all the ships that were taken up were manned by British crews at the time. All foreign crews, despite vociferous protest by some of them, were replaced by British seamen. This restriction also applied to non-British personnel on Royal Naval ships, where, for example, Commonwealth observers on warships were not allowed to stay on board.

A few weeks after the Argentinian surrender, Southampton MP Bob Mitchell commented in the House of Commons that 'the Falkland Islands conflict has clearly shown that the defence of this country requires adequate ships flying under [*sic*] a British flag and staffed by British officers and crew. My contention is that the Merchant Navy should be regarded as an essential part of Britain's defence strategy.' If there were to be another conflict in that region, would the same response by the Merchant Navy now, in 2012, be possible? That question will be examined further in Chapter 9, the Conclusion.

1

The ships

Ships taken up from trade

The Royal Fleet Auxiliary

Ships taken up from trade

When the decision to go to war was taken on 2 April 1982, among the orders issued were powers to use merchant ships – in the exact phrase, 'to take them up from trade'. These powers had existed for some time, in case of emergency, and so could be rapidly enacted. The ships that were chosen were known as STUFT – 'ships taken up from trade'. Some were chartered and some were requisitioned, as necessary.

To support the Royal Navy in the Falklands war, 52 ships from 33 different companies were taken over by the government. In addition, 22 Royal Fleet Auxiliary (RFA) ships and two Royal Maritime Auxiliary Service (RMAS) ships, all crewed by Merchant Navy personnel, were in support. The roles that were undertaken included troopships, hospital ships, aircraft and ammunition carriers, helicopter carriers, repair ships, minesweepers, support ships, dispatch vessels and tugs. Approximately 70 per cent of all the ships involved in the Falklands War were manned by the Merchant Navy.

The various classes of ships all played distinctive roles in the operation, each contributing a vital part to keep the logistical effort moving forward. For example, the thirteen tankers were not closely involved in the fighting, but they made a vital contribution in ensuring that the ships, aircraft and machinery in the land battle ashore had fuel to keep them moving, from diesel fuel and heavy fuel oil for the warships to aviation fuel for the aircraft and lubricating oil and antifreeze for the land vehicles.

Of these tankers, eight were BP 'River' class, of 25,000 tons, one was from Shell, the *Eburna*, of 31,000 tons, and in addition to these Panocean, P&O, and Parley Augustsson provided one ship each. Canadian Pacific's *Fort Toronto* was chartered to supply fresh water. These tankers had to learn the skill of replenishment at sea (RAS), transferring fuel from one ship to another while travelling side-by-side, close, connected by a pipeline in the open ocean. The record for the longest ever fuelling took place at this time, when the *British Tamar* supplied the RFA *Plumleaf* with 18,000 tonnes of fuel in over 52 hours in conditions which were deteriorating to gale force. P&O's *Anco*

Charger spent 42 days continuously at sea, running out of fresh provisions before anchoring in San Carlos Water.

The BP tankers also became involved in ferrying survivors from ships of the Task Force. After the sinking of HMS *Sheffield*, the *British Esk* took her crew back to Ascension Island, with a total of over 300 people on board – a far cry from her normal crew of 31. The *British Tay*, the *British Test*, the *British Dart* and the *British Trent* were also involved in taking survivors away from the Falklands.

There was no opportunity for damaged ships to return to port for repair, so the ships to carry out repairs at sea were found amongst the specialist vessels built for the offshore oil industry. The *Stena Seaspread* and the *Stena Inspector* were two such. Each had five propellers, enabling them to move in any desired direction, and they had a range of 21,000 miles without the necessity to refuel. They were equipped with a dynamic positioning system which enabled them to keep their position automatically with an accuracy of 3 metres in winds up to severe gale force 9 and a stabilising system which reduced their roll by up to 75 per cent.

In some cases, damaged ships would need to be towed to sheltered waters before they could be repaired. With this in mind, three tugs were added to the ships taken up. All three belonged to United Towing Ltd of Hull. The largest, the *Salvageman*, was, in addition to towing, also designed for oil-rig support work. The other two, the *Irishman* and *Yorkshireman*, although smaller in size, were equally as capable. The *Irishman* was involved in the attempted salvage of the *Atlantic Conveyor*, and was towing her until the latter sank, parting the tow.

The campaign could not have been undertaken without adequate aircraft, and in order to transport aircraft to the Falklands additional capacity, over and above the Royal Navy's aircraft carriers, was urgently required. To this end four ships were converted to become aircraft and helicopter carriers. Three of these, the *Atlantic Causeway*, the *Contender Bezant* and the *Astronomer*, carried out their tasks and returned safely. However the fourth, the *Atlantic Conveyor*, did not, as she was hit by Exocet missiles and sank with the loss of twelve lives including the master, Captain Ian North. The *Astronomer* was taken up to replace the loss of the *Atlantic Conveyor*, but by the time that she had been converted, and then reached the Falklands, the Argentinians had surrendered.

There were also stores ships, which were in addition to the dry-stores ships of the RFA. Most of these were chosen because they had their own craneage, but there was also one ro-ro (roll-on/roll-off) ferry. The sister ships *Laertes* and *Lycaon* were taken up for ammunition, primarily, and other stores. Three refrigerated cargo ships were also taken: the *Saxonia* from Cunard, the *Geestport* from the Geest line and the *Avelona Star* from Blue Star Line. The *Tor Caledonia*, from Tor Lloyd, was a ro-ro ship with a stern ramp, and was used for loading vehicles and other equipment. The *Strathewe*, from P&O, was taken to carry construction equipment and materials and two cargo lighters as deck cargo. *Cedarbank*, of Andrew Weir's Bank Line, arrived with stores after the ceasefire, nearly going aground in a severe gale and causing significant damage to the tug *Yorkshireman*, which was trying to tow her to safety.

A British Telecom cable ship, the *Iris*, was taken up as a 'dispatch' vessel, which in naval terms is a general-purpose ship which carries out various tasks that are not required of naval vessels. Although *Iris* was relatively small, at under 4000 tons, her particular design and control systems meant that the weather conditions around the Falklands would not have caused her any significant difficulty in her varied role, carrying passengers and stores as required.

The RMS *St Helena*, which normally operated to and from Cape Town to the UK by way of St Helena and Ascension, was the subject of a very thorough conversion to enable her to become a depot ship for two Hunt class minehunters.[1] Among other changes to her normal state, she was armed with four 20 mm cannons and machine guns, and a flight deck for a helicopter.

The *Wimpey Seahorse* was, at the time, one of the largest

---

[1] These had arrived to relieve the converted deep sea trawlers *Cordella*, *Junella*, *Farnella* and *Pict*, which had been taken up but had been manned by Royal Naval crews (under protest from their normal crew) because of the dangers involved in mine sweeping. They had operated without a depot ship.

anchor-handling tugs ever built in the UK, but was given a very particular role as a mooring vessel, laying buoys in the sheltered bays of South Georgia and at the Falklands themselves for the ships that needed these facilities. She took with her, on her journey south, a total of some 700 tons of deck cargo. She encountered particularly bad weather on the way, with winds up to hurricane force 12.

Troopships were, of course, a vital part of the force. The first to be chosen was the *Canberra*, which could carry 3000 troops. The *Norland*, a North Sea ferry that normally ran from Hull to Rotterdam, was also chosen for her considerable capacity. Accompanying them, to take the military stores and equipment, including tanks, were the *Elk* and the *Europic Ferry*, both of which were roll-on/roll-off ferries. Three more of these also taken up: the *Nordic Ferry*, the *Baltic Ferry* and the *St Edmund*. The *Queen Elizabeth II*, also part of the fleet, took her troops to South Georgia, dodging icebergs as she approached. The *Uganda*, a British India liner, had her role changed from an educational cruise ship to a hospital ship. At that time she had a thousand schoolchildren on board, who all had to leave in Naples, ending their holiday early.[2] Her conversion involved being painted in white with large red crosses on her sides and funnel and the installation of full hospital facilities, including operating theatres, intensive care units and all the other departments necessary.

The Royal Fleet Auxiliary

The Royal Fleet Auxiliary was totally involved. All of its 27 ships were activated for use, and 22 were operating in support of the Task Force.

The RFA is a civilian-manned fleet of ships, owned by the Ministry of Defence. It is distinct from the Merchant Navy, although it is manned by certificated Merchant Navy officers, engineers and crew. The RFA fleet is designed specifically for the task of supporting the Royal Navy, and in 1982 it included

---

[2] It is alleged they went off singing 'Rule Britannia'.

fleet replenishment ships such as the *Fort Grange* and the *Fort Austin*, a variety of replenishment tankers of various sizes, from the large *Olmeda* to the smaller *Blue Rover*, and the six landing ships *Sir Geraint*, *Sir Percivale*, *Sir Tristram*, *Sir Bedivere*, *Sir Lancelot* and *Sir Galahad*. Of these, the *Sir Galahad* is probably the most well known, for she was heavily bombed, with many casualties among the crew and the Welsh Guards who were on board at the time. She was subsequently taken to sea and sunk as a war grave.

The primary role of the RFA is to support the Royal Navy, and thus when the Task Force set out on 6 April the first two ships that were ready to go accompanied them. They were the fleet tanker *Olmeda*, of 25,000 tons, and the *Resource*, a large replenishment ship of about 18,000 tons, carrying solid stores such as food and ammunition. The other ships very rapidly followed. The *Stromness* was restored with food stores and armament, and embarked 300 Royal Marines; she sailed, fully loaded, on 11 April. Some of the ships were diverted from operations elsewhere in the world; the *Fort Austin*, *Tidespring* and *Appleleaf* were in the Mediterranean on exercises. As the *Fort Austin* was near Gibraltar she was the first to reach Ascension Island, the *Tidespring* arriving the day after.

All the RFA ships were worked to their utmost. For example, the *Olmeda* carried out 185 replenishments at sea, a highly specialised and potentially dangerous operation transferring the liquid cargo to warships, and receiving fuel oil from the Merchant Navy tankers for onward transfer. For the *Olmeda* and the warships that she supplied this was a regular occurrence, but for the tankers that were supplying her and her sister ships it was an entirely new and exciting (!) experience, to the extent that RFA officers were seconded to assist in these operations.

The amphibious landing ships mentioned above, supported by the *Europic Ferry*, were in place for landings on 21 May, by which time ships were in San Carlos Water to begin further unloading. Air attacks during the day resulted in the *Fort Austin* being credited with the first 'kill' by an RFA ship, bringing down a Mirage jet fighter. By the end of May, 21 of the RFA fleet were operating in the area south of Ascension Island.

With only a few exceptions the ships of the Royal Navy, the

Royal Fleet Auxiliary and the Merchant Navy all worked harmoniously together. The Royal Navy could not have succeeded without the support of the other two organisations. The crews on the merchant ships had virtually no experience of working with the Navy, and virtually no training, apart from those who were members of the Royal Naval Reserve, but as on so many previous occasions, accompanied by grumbles and mutters, they set to and adapted to their changing surroundings and circumstances.

The accounts in the following chapters are taken from those who served in some of the ships that have been briefly described in this chapter. The ships represented are a cross-section, and the accounts are from differing perspectives, each focusing on the particular individual's role on that ship. They give a wide panorama of what was experienced by merchant seamen at the time of the Falklands War. That time, for some, ended more or less when the war did. For others the task continued well beyond the end of hostilities, supporting the troops and providing facilities.

2

The liners

Canberra

Uganda

Canberra

The *Canberra* was one of the icons of the Falklands war. She had been built at the Harland and Wolff shipyard, Belfast, in 1961 and cost £17 million. With her twin, side-by-side, funnels she was instantly recognisable. She had been built to take advantage of the assisted passage scheme to Australia for emigrants, the 'Ten Pound Pom' scheme as it became known. However, the rapid increase in air travel in the early 1960s reduced the demand for regular passenger liners, and at the same time fuel costs increased considerably. So, like many other ships, *Canberra* became a cruise liner until she was finally scrapped in 1997. Her engines were of an unusual type for the time, as she had twin turbo electric engines, with steam turbines powering electric engines which powered twin propellers. These engines initially gave her 27 knots, but 20 years later her top speed was said to be 23 knots. In so doing, she consumed up to 300 tons of fuel per day. As a cruise liner she carried over 1700 passengers and had 795 officers and crew. As a troopship, she carried very many more.

The chief officer's tale

Captain Martin Reed was the chief officer of *Canberra* when she was taken up from trade. She was, at the time, returning to Southampton from a world cruise. Passing Gibraltar, a party of military planners joined the ship, their purpose, unbeknown to the passengers, to assess the alterations that needed to be made for her new use.

They were in Southampton for two days while two flight decks were fitted, stores were loaded and all the troops were embarked. A volunteer British crew had taken over from the regular Indian and Pakistani crew.

A ship full of troops is a very different proposition to a ship of fare-paying passengers. However, the troops:

> ... took great care of the ship. Some parts suffered, of course. The washing machines in the accommodation, normally used for passengers' scanties, tended to collapse

under continuous full-load running; the composition surface of the promenade deck began to disintegrate under 4000 man-miles of daily running; our beautiful bone-white teak decking reacted badly to gun oil and mortar base plates.[1]

The ship's crew was trained to transfer troops by various methods to a variety of assault craft, whether by helicopter or landing craft. The Merchant Navy crew became accustomed to a new daily routine, which included the use of defensive armament:

Once the military had left the ship we needed volunteers to man our machine guns. I eventually had 50 trained (?) machine gunners ready from all parts of the ship to take over our defence. Heaven help the opposition!

Replenishment at sea became a familiar practice. They refuelled seven times from RFA tankers and transferred stores on many more occasions by various methods, including by helicopter. Martin Reed remembers one particular RAS:

Whilst we toddled along at 10–12 knots, HMSs *Active*, *Ambuscade*, *Alacrity* and *Minerva* successively fuelled from *Olna*'s starboard side. One of my distinct memories of this RAS was after dark. The distance line markers and the hoses were marked with Cyalume pencils, green chemical lights, giving a beautiful soft glow whilst the RAS parties on *Olna* and *Canberra* had their lifejacket lights switched on (we always wore lifejackets on the RAS point) all twinkling away like overlarge fireflies. Both ships were completely blacked-out; with just the sound of the sea between this and the gentle lights it was a scene of intense beauty – quite unforgettable.

As they approached the Falklands, and then San Carlos Water, on 21 May for the main landing of the invasion force, tensions

---

[1] Extracts from Martin Reed's account were published in the *Naval Review*, October 1983, and in J. Winton, *Signals From the Falklands*, London, 1995. Reproduced here with permission of the *Naval Review*.

rose on board:

> I can recollect the hair lifting on the back of my neck as we slid past the silhouette of Fanning Head early that morning; we had been briefed that the Argentinians were on Fanning and could be a problem ... The first air attack came at 08.50 in beautiful weather conditions. From the bridge we saw a Pucara aircraft come racing around Fanning Head, launch a salvo of rockets at HMS *Argonaut*, and turn in towards the anchorage and us! I am quite sure that we were the first ship in San Carlos Water to open fire with our machine guns and Blowpipe missiles as the plane veered away down our port side, over the headland and away. I remember turning to the First Officer and saying, 'I don't know about you, but my hands are shaking!' 'Don't worry,' he replied, 'so are mine!'

Later that day they had a sobering task:

> When the dusk fell I had the very moving experience of bringing the survivors of HMS *Ardent* on board; wet cold and shocked, their bearing and discipline were magnificent and they deserve the highest praise ... Late on Friday we disembarked the *Ardent* survivors to HMS *Leeds Castle*. Led by a piper from the Scots Guards, we led them down through the galley and out along a brow through the shell doors. Hundreds, then thousands, lined the rails to shout and sing their farewell. Our Royal Marine band formed up of its own accord on the promenade deck and all work stopped as it played and sang our adopted heroes off their temporary home.

After a period steaming in the holding the zone, some 200 miles from Port Stanley they heard of the ceasefire ashore. Their next task was to repatriate Argentinian prisoners of war, 4144 of them. So that the *Canberra* would be identified as having them on board, screens were hung over the side, visible from the air, with the letters PW. They were safely delivered to Puerto Madryn in Argentina, where the *Canberra* was met by an Argentinian warship, the *Santísima Trinidad*, a type 42 destroyer

– the same class as HMS *Sheffield* but built in Argentina. Ironically, the *Santísima Trinidad* had been at the forefront of the Falklands invasion, carrying the naval and army senior officers.

The *Canberra* was away for 94 days and covered 27,187 miles. Among other statistics, by the time the ship returned her crew had served 646,847 meals and treated 172 casualties, of which 82 were British and 90 Argentinian. Six weeks after her return to Southampton the traditional crew had returned and she was back in normal service with more peaceful passengers.

The electrical officer's tale

Don Cole, who was a second electrical officer on board *Canberra*, wrote this account some years later, but it remained unpublished. Prompted by his friend Malcolm Orr (see Chapter 4, *British Trent*), he contributed his memories for this book. He had joined the ship in January 1982 and was on board when, towards the end of her world cruise, she passed Gibraltar and the military advisers boarded.

> The next day we were briefed by Captain Scott-Masson and a Royal Navy Captain Burns, who had joined us at Gibraltar, that the ship was being taken up from service and placed under the control of the RN captain in preparation for the transportation of British military troops to the Falkland Islands ... A certain amount of 'let's go and get 'em' emerged amongst the crew ... Mixed with the realisation after being told we would be asked to volunteer to make the trip ... we would have to sign on under a different set of rules that apply in a war scenario.

He telephoned home to tell his parents. Not unnaturally, his mother was worried and upset that he had volunteered. He had his own concerns:

> More worrying to me personally was the news that the Argentine navy had some fairly useful ships including submarines which I think a lot of Merchant Navy crew feared the most. I had worked on many submarines during my apprenticeship at Vickers in Barrow and knew what

submarines and torpedoes are capable of, and as I would be spending much of the time 'down below' on the main switchboard 32 feet below the waterline, I was a little worried to say the least.

He was involved with the conversion of the ship for her role as a troop carrier, for the men of 3 Para and the Royal Marines, who were shortly to join them. The conversion works included the drilling of the handrails for machine-gun mountings. They sailed in the evening of Good Friday with few witnesses to their departure – other than the band of the Parachute Regiment playing them off on the quayside. As with the other ships, they settled into a new routine, but the troops' training added a new dimension:

The troops did small arms training, shooting bin bags floating away from the galley dump each day, lectures on survival techniques and the best way to cut a sheep's throat, there were a lot of sheep on the Falklands, keeping fit and running mile after mile around the promenade deck, which was normally used by passengers walking off lunch.

As they steamed south a sports day was organised for the troops and crew. Included in the programme was a 10 km race to be run round the promenade deck.

The race was open to all on board, and the finest athletes from all services were there, plus Frank the laundry man who was our secret weapon. Frank was an excellent distance runner who did marathons for fun. Frank stormed the race and left all the embarked forces in his slipstream.

When *Canberra* arrived at Ascension Island, she anchored and awaited the arrival of other ships.

It was at Ascension that I saw, for the last time but not the first, HMS *Sheffield*, a type 42 destroyer. She was built in Barrow by me and a few others in the mid-70s and I had even been on sea trials with her. She was my first time at sea and I think what inspired me to seek a career at sea. I remember standing on her aft mooring deck during the speed trials in the Clyde Firth in Scotland and not being able to see anything but a wall of white foaming water all around the aft end as she hit full speed with her twin Olympus gas turbines screaming away at full power.

After eventually sailing from Ascension, *Canberra* became part of the Battle Group, together with *Atlantic Conveyor* and *Norland*, with a destroyer escort and, although it was not known at the time, HM Submarine *Spartan* below them. As they progressed south, into the South Atlantic winter, the weather became colder. This produced some slightly unusual side effects:

In the cold of the South Atlantic one of our helicopters developed a starting problem, which was causing some concern as it was needed for flying operations. As luck would have it our engineers were dab hands at starting troublesome lifeboat engines and came to the rescue with a tin or two of 'easy start' in the helicopter's engine air intake, which did the trick.

They were able to keep up to date with events, as the BBC World Service was broadcast to all cabins, despite, on the *British Trent*, Malcolm Orr's scepticism of the news that was being broadcast.

On 20 May, they went to full alert at 22.00 as they prepared to enter Falkland Sound; the ship was totally blacked out. Days had been spent in preparation for this, ensuring that all the external lighting had been disabled and all the windows and ports had been completely screened.

I was on the main switchboard during the arrival in the Sound, keeping an eye on the ship's load as she was driven and manoeuvred by huge electric propulsion motors. If we had lost electrical power at this stage there would have been no landings on that day in May, but *Canberra* was a very well-maintained ship.

He was on duty most of the night, returning to his cabin at 09.00 the next morning. He then went out on deck with a colleague to have a look round:

> ... dressed in our white boiler suits. We had only taken a few steps onto the open flight deck, when we were told by the flight deck officer that we would make an easy target for an enemy sniper, dressed in white. A good point well delivered so we went back inside again.

Returning to the engine room in case he was needed, by 11.00 he could hear the sound and then the smell of exploding bombs. Relieved from his station before lunch by another electrical officer, and unsuccessfully seeking some lunch:

> I made my way aft along to the aft mooring deck to sneak a look 'over the wall' and to try and get some air to wake myself up a bit. There were helicopters flying around all over the Bay and I could see smoke from HMS *Ardent* that had received a pounding from the Argentine air force. I was only there a few minutes when from over a hill I saw a small piston-engine plane (a Pucara ground attack aircraft) ... with tracer fire from our defences streaking towards it. Time to get back inside!

Shortly after that, the survivors from HMS *Ardent* and other ships were boarding, among them:

> ... the walking wounded, guys in shock, blackened faces from the ships they had tried to defend. They spend a few days on board wandering around feeling helpless with no purpose, dressed in white boiler suits as they had nothing else to wear, as all their belongings had been lost on their ships.

They left Falkland Sound shortly after that to proceed to the holding area, where, like other ships, they steamed around an 'imaginary box'. As is mentioned in Malcolm Orr's account from the *British Trent*, for the *Canberra's* crew this was also a low point in their deployment, steaming round in cold grey conditions waiting for something to happen. They were then sent to rendezvous with the *Queen Elizabeth 2* in South Georgia to receive more troops to take to the beachhead in San Carlos Water. There was some resentment that the *QE2* was deemed too valuable to risk, but the Scots and Welsh Guards embarked and disembarked in San Carlos Water from the *Canberra* without incident.

> We re-entered San Carlos Bay and dropped anchor. We're back, have another go if you want. Nothing, not even a single shot fired the second time around. Dropped the troops off again. It is getting too easy, piece of cake for veteran troop transporters like us, no job too small, give us a call.

After the Argentinian surrender, the *Canberra* repatriated 3000 prisoners of war to Puerto Madryn in Argentina:

> The majority of the 3000 slept in the large public rooms on *Canberra* and NCOs and officers in cabins. We had to pick up an armed British army escort if we had to enter any area where the POWs were held, which was a bit scary. After disembarking, the passengers, who had been fed and watered, were glad to be home, which is more than can be said for the stern-faced army officers who accepted the transfer [of the prisoners] from the British army officers and the International Red Cross.

For the return trip to the United Kingdom, *Canberra* had embarked over 2000 Royal Marines, including their band. The bandsmen's job in war is as stretcher bearers. However, the band had come with their instruments, so on the way back, they:

> ... put on one of the most memorable events of the whole trip for me, the ceremony of 'Beating the Retreat', which must have so much history and was very appropriate as we were heading away from all that had gone before. On a balmy summer's evening steaming across a flat calm Bay of Biscay with a fabulous sun setting on the port bow, the band of the Royal Marines treated all on board to the most moving open-air concert ever, concluding with the last post played by a solo bugle player.

Two days after that, and after disembarking the Royal Marines at Plymouth, *Canberra* returned to Southampton. Don Cole went up on deck to witness the arrival, together with the majority of the military and ship's crew, all on the starboard side:

> This caused quite a list to starboard, which had to be corrected by the engineers ballasting the ship. I found a gap in the line of crew and wedged myself in and witnessed a truly amazing welcome home ... There was hardly any space between the mass of large and small craft milling around the ship as we edged ever closer to *Canberra*'s berth, her home.

Don Cole wrote his account 25 years after the event, and he noted that although some of the details were hazy, much was still very clear to him. Many events of those days remain so.

The assistant purser's journal

Lauraine Mulberry was the acting deputy purser, one of the small number of female staff on board who remained on the ship for her deployment. During that period she kept a detailed journal, with an introduction which was written en route to the Falklands. The main part of the journal starts on 21 May and finishes on 8 June. As one of the few women on board she had a different perspective to the events of that time. The introduction gives a clear pointer to her state of mind. The journal then follows. It is reproduced here almost in its entirety.

> It is so incongruous to sit here in the office and glance out of the window and see a soldier in camouflage jacket carrying a complete backpack and gun. Normally one would see a middle-aged grey-haired passenger gazing lazily over the rail at the sea. The incongruity of eating dinner – with a string quartet – to hear conversation of cold storage for bodies and then the conversation turn, casually, to the poetry of Yeats and Wordsworth. The ship is full of sharp contrast: warship/cruise ship; helicopter pad/swimming pool; operating theatre/nightclub. This is so totally real and yet surreal. Cruising will, quite literally,

never be the same. You will constantly see behind the frivolous facade of a cruise the darkness of men gearing themselves for a fight and possibly even death. What is remarkable is the perfect function of *Canberra* in her present role: she is a warship. To accommodate 2000 fighting men and their equipment, to give them a training ground, to facilitate helicopter landings seems almost her normal function. But what sadness if she becomes a hospital ship – taking broken men and lives back to their homes and waiting families. What feelings will then permeate the ship; how can one accept cruising after that? This is for a principle, a right – but at what a price.

21 May

We spent the 20th at sea with the rest of the Task Force in heavy seas and cold biting wind – all heading towards Stanley. Quite an impressive sight – some 38 ships in convoy. From 10 p.m. the ship went to Emergency Stations as we, in a convoy of six ships, broke away and headed for San Carlos. The ship was made watertight and all on board stayed in public rooms close to their [life] boat. We anchored at 12.45 – slow going as there was a possibility of mines and we had no minesweepers.

Assault forces from the other ships went ashore at 2.30 a.m. on the 21st. Camp beds were put out in the bureau and we actually slept. There was shelling from one of our ships in the early hours – sounded quite muffled where we were. Breakfast was at 6 and from 8.45 onwards we were constantly diving for cover from spasmodic air attacks. The bay is full of the Task Force; we have guns mounted on the bridge wing and 'blow pipes' on the officers deck. Had a walk around the open deck at 6.45 am, 21st, a lovely clear morning – a sliver of the moon and landing craft busily making their way ashore. You could see tracer fire on the closest point – Fanning Point.

Also this morning we started our medical role and

admitting all casualties on board. We are taking it in four-hour shifts; we have to write down all the known details and then interview the patient for any missing facts. We are also awaiting 42 refugees from San Carlos settlement but because of the air raids they are being delayed – seems they are women and children. Casualties have been coming in by helicopter but how many I don't know. Seems 3 Para, who were sent to take the highest ridge surrounding San Carlos Bay, have encountered more resistance than they expected – possibly tanks – so 42 Commando have now been sent ashore to help. The idea is to hold the complete bay and to make it safe for the Task Force therein and to stop any routes for troops of the Argentines to come across from Stanley.

We have just heard that HMS *Antrim*, which is 200 yards off us, has taken an unexploded bomb. She is transferring casualties over to us and then heading out to sea. Seems someone will have to try and defuse it ...

2.30 p.m. – Further air attack has put out *Argonaut* – badly damaged – and *Ardent* is so badly hurt we are expecting her complement to transfer over to us – not very good for a day to start. Hopefully with darkness at 4 p.m. things may go quiet. Sally and John have just finished their rota – now three dead, six [patients] in Bonito Ward and an unknown number awaiting surgery. Helen and I have spent most of the day either under a table in the Bonito area or under the desk in the bureau resting on lifejackets – quite comfortable in a strange way. If the Bonito Ward fills up too quickly the medicos will also have to utilise the Meridian Room. Helen and I are on duty again at 6 p.m. At 5 p.m. we embarked the 150-odd survivors from *Ardent* – out of 170. Had nothing except what they stood up in.

22 May

Helen and I worked until 7.15 p.m. for dinner, actually

feeding patients and washing them and talking to them, then came back up until 8.30 p.m. double-checking our admission figures as they would be sent to London that night – 23 in intensive care including 3 Argentines who are very young, very filthy and frostbitten. One chap had two shots through both eyes – a Royal Marine – many pitiful sights. Went to cabin to have the pleasure of taking off uniform, showering and washing hair. A yellow alert on aircraft came through at 9.25, back on went uniform and waited until 9.50 to hear the threat had diminished – off clothes and into bed – slept from 1 a.m. to 3.30 a.m. when another yellow alert for aircraft was received – nothing happened so out of uniform again only to be followed at 5.20 a.m. by a fire party investigation which ended in nothing at 6 a.m. – disturbed night but a great relief from the day.

It was decided last night to put [the remainder of] 42 Commando ashore and for us to sail out of the Bay whilst the going was good. A lot of gear and men to get off. It was hoped to be outside the 200 mile WZ by 5 a.m. today but we were late sailing due to *Stromness* and we had to cut down on speed to keep with her and crippled *Antrim* who is with us. At 9 p.m. we were still 100 miles within the zone steaming northwest of the Falklands. We now have four dead onboard – all Gazelle pilots and crew. The minor injuries (about 40) have moved from Island Room to Meridian for greater safety.

23 May

Actually spent a civilised quiet evening; changed into my blue dress (brazen) a drink before dinner, a leisurely dinner, a drink after dinner in the Cricketers. Sat with a young helicopter pilot with a broken ankle. He was piloting the SAS on the Pebble Beach raid – 25 SAS men – completed raid – no injuries and when flying between ships with them the helicopter plunged into the sea – 20 of the SAS men drowned – he only of the crew escaped and is now living in agony of guilt and remorse – all that to cope with at 23 years of age. There is talk of us going back into San Carlos tonight; the *Ardent* survivors don't wish to and neither do the patients. (Crew ain't too happy! – 150% or not!) However, come this morning, all ammo, supplies and remnants of 3 Para, 40/42 Commando are being transferred to the stores ship *Resource* so perhaps she is going in and we will be reprieved. So far this morning (10.30) we have had only two new casualties flown in. We have our own Wessex 'hospital' helicopter ...

We (APs) are having a purser type day. We have had to enter and check every cabin on board (1000) as the berthing done by the transport and movements major had become so chaotic and if we are doing the rest and recreation (eventually) we need to be in a position to know what we have. Low-dependency patients will also be going into cabins from the Meridian Room 'hospital'.

25 May

We are now 200 miles west of Stanley and steaming for South Georgia where, we believe, we will rendezvous with *QE2* and probably take on her troops. The survivors of *Antelope* are now on *Norland* and it is thought that they and [the survivors of] *Ardent*, plus well-enough patients we are carrying, will go over to *QE2* and she will probably head for Ascension and then home. We have heard that *Uganda* is anchored in West Falkland by international agreement between UK and Argentine Red Cross so at long last she will start playing a useful role. The helicopter activity has been horrendous – every passing ship gets our ammo and stores. We are transferring a field surgery team to *Hydra* today and they will set up shop in Ajax Bay – a bit further down than we were. Obviously needed in the big push towards Stanley. The shoreside seems to be going extremely well from all reports. Just wonder when it will be all over and at what cost. *Hydra* actually came alongside with difficulty due to a large swell and took off six patients. Argentine news reports state that we have sunk – obviously didn't realise that we had sailed away under the cover of darkness or else some pilot missed his target but claimed a hit!

27 May

We are now steaming around South Georgia – bitterly cold – awaiting the arrival of *QE2*. Seems she is in fog and ice some 100 miles away and is now due to rendezvous with us tomorrow. We and *Norland* are taking half each of her troops and *QE2* will take *Ardent* and *Antelope* survivors plus some of our patients and beetle back to UK. Had a lovely evening last night – a cocktail party pre-dinner, wine with dinner – we have been 'dry' since the action started – followed by a 'concert' by four members of the Royal Marine band. Most enjoyable and much needed respite from 'war'.

29 May

A rather hectic 36 hours. *QE2* finally arrived off Grytviken at about 6.30 p.m. on the 27th and we took on all the Welsh Guards at 9–1.15 am. Poor things – all this being done in complete darkness and with 90 lb packs and rifles on them. Got up at 06.30 on 28th and walked around the deck. Quite a sight: *QE2* here, the *Norland*, *Leeds Castle* and three converted minesweepers, plus little boats dashing out from Grytviken with M Company of Royal Marines (who retook it) and the British scientific people (their survey ship *Endurance* virtually led us in). At 8 a.m. (28th) we started embarking again – the rest of Five Brigade which includes Scots Guards, Naval Air and Royal Air Force sections and many other minor units. The Gurkhas transferred to the *Norland*. We sailed at 8.15 (past icebergs at the entrance! – something else for me to worry about) today we are in heavy force 8 gale – brilliant sunshine. The prom deck and games decks are bristling with guns ready for our re-entrance into the Falkland Islands.

30 May

Still ploughing our way to the FI – once outside we are to steam in our 'box' again – guarded by HMS *Bristol*. Malcolm's birthday today – his first at sea so celebrated in suitable fashion. Very few at church today – they all had their separate services in various public rooms. The Scots Guards padre addressed our interdenominational service – a very John Knox figure spouting fire and brimstone.

31 May

Seems we may still not 'go in' tonight – the *Elk* and *Atlantic Causeway* are scheduled in (*Elk* is chock-a-block with ammo); evidently 'they' want *Norland* to go in – because she is the prisoner ship – to collect the 1400 prisoners. However if she doesn't arrive in the 'box' by nightfall (3 p.m.-ish) then we will go to drop off what we can. Lots of helicopter activity today – with quite a few ships in the 'box'. Outward mail is being taken off to *Argonaut* who is going to limp her way home to UK. 11.40 – yellow alert was sounded and all the machine guns crews rushed outside ('close up'). They are still at their station some two hours later – in bitter cold. In direct contrast, we went up to D/C's birthday party ... ! We have now been told we are not going 'in' until 1 June so another hopefully safe night.

1 June

A cold, clear, brilliantly sunny day – gun crews are closed up by 7 am – just in case. Heard on the news that two Exocet missile-carrying planes were actually shot down – good news – they can't have many left – either the missiles themselves (unless they are secretly buying from Libya) or the aeroplanes to carry them. Makes one feel safer. Our business goes on as usual – every day 8 am meeting with the Purser and today I shall take the risk of balancing the safe – must earn my keep and 150 per cent.

11.45 am – we are steaming 'in' accompanied by HMS *Broadsword* and we have just passed *Hermes* going the other way! Plans are going ahead for this evening's disembarkation and possible embarkation of casualties. Looks as though we shall be in the bureau from 10 p.m. until anchorage (about midnight) – purser is planning a cribbage match!

2 June

A lovely, misty, rainy day. Arrived in Ajax Bay area around 4 a.m. (went to general emergency stations) and anchored at 5.30 a.m. Went back to bed at 6.15 a.m. until 8 a.m. The 5th Brigade are now busy scrabbling with landing craft and helicopters are busy taking off supplies. The area is full of ships – barely visible in the mist. *Norland* is here still taking off prisoners. It is going to be a long and hopefully uneventful day. Constant disembarking of troops and gear by landing craft plus our ship's launches. However didn't get it all ashore so we decided to stay the night in the Bay. *Fearless* and 5/6 other ships are here as well.

Took on wounded at 11.30 – eighteen Argentinians, three 2 Para and one RM. The Argentinians are all in the Bonito Ward under guard with machine gun as there are several commando Argentinian officers – really tough and awkward bunch. One lieutenant's surname is Brown and he was educated at Oxford; another is called Alexander Lopez and has an English mother. The infantry are a different story – mostly Indian peasant type – swarthy skin and thick features – some very young – just eighteen and some badly suffering from malnutrition. The officers are the elite and obviously a different class and breed of people.

We have moved all the English wounded down to the

Meridian Room, to stop any animosity and also infection from gangrene which the Argentinians have. The RM we have in is suffering from frostbite. The Argentine infantry were filthy dirty and one poor soul, very badly wounded, has lain in a trench for three days before being treated. Some of the conflicting stories are quite incredible and some possibly true. The wounds are entirely different from our first experience – these are bullet and shrapnel – chest and stomach wounds. The wounds are all left open – just a pad dressing on them – to stop infection and then are sewn up in 2/3 days' time.

3 June

A quiet night – no air raid and another misty morning. Lots of helicopter activity from the ships to the shore. We will sail at 6 p.m. today and should spend tomorrow in a 'box' at sea, RAS (fuel and food) ...

8 June

All very quiet – we are still loitering in our area – called TRALA (tug, repair and loitering [logistics] area). We are being supplied with beer and some supplies from RFA ships and we have taken on 2900 tons of oil by RAS. Of the few left on board – mostly medical – they are becoming very bored. There has been no news of Stanley from the BBC or anywhere else so everything is dependent on that. *QE2* has gone home with the survivors of *Ardent*, *Coventry* and *Argonaut* plus our patients. We will either be sent to South Georgia or perhaps into the sound next to Stanley once the heavy fighting is over or back to San Carlos – at the moment – no one knows.

Although her journal ends there, she also wrote a letter to friends from Port Stanley on 25 June, eleven days after the Argentinian surrender. This described the events of the days following the close of her journal:

Well, the first thing to say is that we are expected back in Southampton on Sunday 11 July at 11 a.m. This is of course dependent on further orders from Min of Defence regarding speed and course. We don't appear to be stopping anywhere en route but will perhaps go close to Ascension Island to pick up mail and/or fresh goodies and to go close to Las Palmas so that the P&O technical people may board in preparation of drydock specifications. Cannot believe it and probably won't until we get there ...

You all no doubt heard about our POW run from San Carlos to Port Stanley and thence to the Argentine mainland with 4200 prisoners. We stripped cabins of mattresses and bedding – they all had one pillow and that is all; cabins were filled to capacity for beds and thence 2/3 on the floor where possible and then the public rooms were used. The embarkation took all night and there was a queue of POW walking from the airport into Stanley and thence by boat to us – an all-night affair. Many were well dressed in uniforms plus blankets and sleeping bags; there were a few cases of undernourishment but not many; several cases of lice, scabies and much dysentery. They were fed with two meals a day and each meal took five hours to complete (e.g. from 7 to 12 and then re-feeding all over again from 3 until 8 p.m.). We had only 200 guards – made up of Welsh Guards who were blown off *Sir Galahad* and a company of 3 Para.

It was quite bizarre arriving in Puerto Madryn; no civilians in sight; plenty of coaches for the POWs (like a shore excursion arrival); ambulances for the injured and a colonel of some description who shook hands with the injured and the officers and then went away. We had an Argentinian frigate escort in and out which was slightly unnerving but the whole thing seemed so improbable. It was hard to believe that we had been fighting each other for three weeks and then brought them back to their home on a mini cruise.

We fully expected to have to take a further 2000 but were very pleasantly surprised to find on our arrival back that there were only our own troops to embark. It has taken some time to sort out who goes on what and where and when – plenty of arguments ashore in various brigade HQs.

I managed to get ashore to take minutes of the meeting – a dismal place that has been cleaned up immensely since the Argentina departure. Locals leave a lot to be desired and talk about the British and the Argentinians so I wonder who they think they are and who they belong to. We were told not to stray off the main road as there are so many mines and booby traps around – wounded from these are still coming in each day. It kept on showering; low clouds everywhere and quite cold. The troops are living in houses, tents and portable cabins; peat is the only source of fuel and generators for light are hard to come by. Water is a serious problem on the island and many troops were living in unsanitary conditions. In the anchorage with us are many merchant ships awaiting troops to take home and *Uganda* who is acting as the hospital for the island. She is staying a while longer until a ship arrives from UK with hospital equipment and until the runway is ready to take Hercules aircraft.

So I suppose it is over – nothing definite seems to have been settled – and all at a cost of 250 dead and many men shattered mentally and physically. A high price to pay.

The master's journal

The late Captain Dennis Scott-Masson CBE, ADC was in command of the *Canberra* for her round-the-world voyage in early 1982 and remained in command for her deployment to the Falklands. He started a journal on 3 April and maintained it until her return to the United Kingdom. The journal started before they had returned to Southampton on the round-the-world voyage.

As they passed Gibraltar on 4 April they stopped off the Breakwater to allow Captain Bradford RN and a military party on board. He was advised that the ship 'was to be requisitioned to carry 40 and 42 Commando and 3 Para to somewhere near the Falkland Islands.'

The next day:

> No longer did I have time to think ... It was a feat that still the passengers and ship's company did not know what was going on ... however, six or eight close-cropped obviously military-looking men climbing up the pilot ladder at Gibraltar, an unscheduled stop, started a few rumours!

When they arrived in Southampton, the physical changes to the ship started immediately. The captain was involved with 'a constant stream of visitors in and out of my quarters. Naval, military, P&O, DTI and Hogg Robinson, the government representatives. SNO Captain Burns, Commander EMF, Colonel T Seccombe, Royal Marines, joined. Thursday Lord Inchcape arrived to bid us farewell and party in my cabin included all above' – and many others, including his wife Anne-Marie.

On Good Friday, 9 April, they:

> ... embarked 2100 military, of 40 and 42 Royal Marine Commando and 3rd Battalion Parachute Regiment and various ancillary units. Crew 424 – all British and some from the pool (deck and engine). Great reluctance on my part.[2]

They sailed at 20.00, and from his position on the bridge he was aware that:

> ... thousands lined the whole of Southampton Water, the Isle of Wight and Southsea etc ... I remain a little punch-drunk and stunned by the recent events and it is taking time to come to terms with them. When will we be back and under what circumstances?

---

[2] Pool ratings were an unknown quantity, when compared in his mind to the normal P&O Indian crews.

The embarked troops caused some initial difficulties, such as when 20 Royal Marines got into a lift and so overloaded it that it rapidly descended to the bottom and was written off for the duration. The use of all lifts by the troops was immediately banned.

On 13 April he reorganised his deck officers:

> Today I have made Second Officer Lane full-time navigator and promoted Horn to second officer and also Brook to third officer. Signal shown me by SNO, part of the text of which was ' ... P&O officers put to shame some RN officers.'

Like many others, Captain Scott-Masson listened to the BBC World Service and was indignant about the news broadcast on the Merchant Navy Programme (long since discontinued):

> It suggested that when we got south we would hoist the White Ensign[3]. These comments do no good for the morale of the crew and I have to refute them.

On a lighter note, he noted on the same day that the troops:

> ... have been supplied with 5000 French letters. In view of our ultimate destination I queried the need, only to be told they are blown up and used for target practice!

While they were at anchor at Ascension Island, waiting for the fleet to assemble, he discovered that the *Canberra* was very lucky in at least one respect:

> We have no rationing. *Fearless* have fresh water for one hour per day and half a sausage for breakfast.

(Graham Harding, the chief radio officer on board *Canberra*, noted that although there was no menu choice for meals there was, as he put it, good sensible grub all the way. However, there was criticism from a member of the press about the

---

[3] The White Ensign is flown by the Royal Navy. The *Canberra* flew the Blue Ensign, which indicated that a proportion of her officers had commissions in the Royal Naval Reserve. These included the captain, the deputy captain, the chief officer and the first officer.

standard of the food.)[4] HMS *Fearless* did not impress *Canberra's* captain:

> Another briefing on *Fearless* ... I am singularly unimpressed with that ship as we were required to climb aboard by a Jacob's ladder which was positively unsafe and not even a helping hand at the top.

While they were still at Ascension, some of the essential supplies on board took a temporary downward turn when:

> ... last Friday the beer saga started when we discovered that the RAF had half-inched our supply. Days went by without a successful resolution. I instructed our purser to dispatch the Cat. D. P. [catering deputy purser] ashore to procure the necessary on our own account. Where both the Navy and the Royal Marines failed, P&O succeeded. Nigel Horne bought 1200 cases, paid £3900 with his personal cheque, commandeered a Pan Am truck and a LCU [landing craft] and got the beer back to the ship.

The decision as to what time zone should be adopted by the fleet caused some difficulties:

> Sometimes I despair of the Navy and the Military. At a *Fearless* briefing it was decreed that we would remain at Zulu time (GMT). Yes, acceptable to fight the war in Zulu but for shipboard administration and to acclimatise the troops we must operate in the time zone (GMT −4). After pressure from me, we decided to make a unilateral decision and alter our clocks in stages of an hour at night as is customary ... At least we do not get up four hours before daylight and have lunch at 0900 local time. I know we are right.

Machine guns had been mounted in various places, including the bridge wing. He noted that:

---

[4] Graham Harding, 'Don't you know it's all changed?' Unpublished account, February 2002.

They are quite impressive when fired with red tracer and scare the pants off me. I hope they would do the same to an attacking Argentinian.

On 19 May his entry noted that on the previous Saturday 'Active Service Declaration was made ... Which puts us on a war footing.' This was reinforced the following Tuesday, when:

> ... everybody on upper decks has to wear foul weather clothing, anti-flash gear, carry lifejacket (RN style) and gas mask ... The ship is totally darkened and as a consequence, somewhat eerie.

All the ships were now completely darkened at night and sailing without navigation lights as they neared the Falklands. The ship handling at night therefore was very different to that which was customary in peace time:

> 22 ships darkened with no navigation lights charging about on a very dark night is highly dangerous. I have just left the bridge after a near collision with *Stromness* and *Appleleaf* during their RAS ... It was fortunate that my officer of the watch, Alan Wilson, was very much on the ball.

Captain Scott-Masson's journal entry for Saturday 22 May is reproduced here in full:

> The events of the past 48 hours have been exciting and different! Also, personally, and I believe I speak for most of the ship's company, somewhat unexpected. Originally stealth of approach to San Carlos and the Sound was aided by bad weather with low cloud, drizzle and poor visibility. However, the final approach was made in perfect weather with good visibility and little wind and a nearly cloudless sky. The Sound between the East and West Falkland Islands was made about 22.00 on Thursday 20th and with all darkened ships, led by HMS *Plymouth*, *Norland*, ourselves and *Stromness* crept through the channel and anchored in the sound at 210045 [0045 on 21 May].
>
> Weighed anchor at 210515 and proceeded into San Carlos Bay to be anchored again at 210600, which we did

on the dot. It was very quiet in the first light and no one guessed what lay ahead and how the tranquillity was soon to be shattered. An almost perfect dawn broke over the islands and the first impression I had of the Falkland Islands was different to what had been imagined. As a result of the good weather the islands appeared benign and not too unwelcoming. As far as the Islanders [were concerned], of course, we were very welcome, as was to be demonstrated during the day.

Not long after our arrival, as the light increased, the first 'air threat red' sounded throughout the ship followed quickly by 'take cover' 'take cover'. A Pucara was seen to be firing cannon at one of the protecting frigates in the Sound and then wheeled to have a go at the ships in the anchorage. A fairly hair-raising experience for everybody and a precursor of what was to follow until sunset. Our efforts at retaliation were quite impressive, as described by 'Uncle Tom',[5] now in *Fearless* with a good view, with our bridge-mounted machine guns and captain's deck 'Blowpipe' firing continuously and dramatically at the enemy aircraft.

As the day progressed we heard of damage to our own ships confined to the RN guarding the entrance to San Carlos Bay. However, the worst was to come with the news of the afternoon that HMS *Ardent* was a blazing inferno and had to be abandoned with her survivors being transferred to us by *Yarmouth*. They lost 20+ of the crew. Alan West, her CO, was a very shocked man – not unsurprisingly.

All day during the raids we unloaded ammunition and equipment and finally our reserve force of 42 Commando were asked to help 2 Para who were having a little trouble with a small pocket of resistance. About 20.30 we received a signal to proceed to sea at 22.30 with *Norland, Europic*

---

[5] Colonel T. Seccombe, Royal Marines.

Ferry with *Antrim* which had lost her weapon system and had two unexploded bombs on board. *Stromness* joined us later.

There was an enormous effort before weighing anchors to get as much equipment ashore as possible and my ship's company unstintingly volunteered to assist as they have done throughout this deployment. Throughout the day the crew were magnificent and rose to every occasion admirably. At the height of the activity I walked around the ship and stoically, with courage and good humour they responded to the repeated loud speaker cries 'take cover'. In the bureau, where I happened to be on one such occasion, the girls calmly once again took their lifejackets and placed themselves in the kneeholes of the desks. The purser remarked that they were like rabbits each in their own hutch. He had his own bolthole in his office next to the safe until he thought that might not be such a good idea as the safe was a little heavy should it fall on him!

I'm sure we were all relieved to get out of San Carlos Bay with the gratification of knowing we had achieved our objective – to land our 2000+ troops and the equipment without one casualty. The ship was whole too, having survived innumerable air attacks. What good fortune. Although the Argentinians never seemed to select us as a prime target, I will never know why as we must have looked enormous sitting there in the middle of the day with our two, still glistening, yellow funnels. Of course, we were landlocked and it was not easy for the pilots to get a good run at us. The Argentinian pilots were determined, skilful and very brave. I understand a lot of them are British trained, which has its irony. Friday was a day none of us will ever forget.

They had a sad task on the following day:

At 1600 on Saturday we committed to the deep four Royal Marines, one officer and three NCOs who had died in two Gazelle helicopters over the land. A very moving ceremony with the RM band.

He was very critical of the press and the way they described the war. In particular, he commented:

> Into my possession this evening came an article in the *Spectator* written by Max Hastings. It is quite scurrilous and I am sending a copy to John Turner [P&O fleet manager] with instructions to sue the publication and him personally by me. He is a snide bastard – I actually wined and dined the fellow. He should be crucified.

He made further comments on the media in his entry for 29 May:

> The press and the media, including the BBC, are beneath contempt. Today a commentator on the 'Overseas World' said 'a week ago the *Canberra* was not acceptable as a target but now she's politically expendable.' Imagine hearing that if you are sitting on board, or a relative of the ship's company at home. I despise these men ... how mindless they must be.[6]

After their passage to South Georgia to rendezvous with the *Queen Elizabeth 2*, he noted:

> We completed the cross-decking of the Welsh Guards, Scots Guards, and minor units from *QE2* at 2000 last night and sailed from Grytviken for, we presume, San Carlos Bay. Excuse given to put us into the A.O.A. again, and not *QE2*, is that her name is too emotive. This does not impress us very much and there is a little sourness felt.

(Graham Harding, in his account, also stated that there was 'a lot of ill feeling when *QE2* felt unable to assist with any stores – not so much as a box of matches!').[7]

While *Canberra* was at Grytviken, the survivors from *Ardent*

---

[6] Anecdotal evidence received indicates that the *Atlantic Conveyor* and the *Canberra* were indeed considered expendable by the MoD. The term 'Chaff Sierra', meaning chaff ships, was a well-known term in some quarters.

[7] Graham Harding, 'Don't you know it's all changed?', 28.

left to be repatriated on the *QE2*:

> They were a very gallant ship's company. There are so many stories from the ships, on the land and in the air of gallantry, bravery and devotion to duty of heroic proportions that it is impossible to record them all. In the Task Force all the finest traditions of all three services, reflecting the best of the British character is readily apparent. Why does it take a war to unite the country? Without reservation I will say that this is the finest body of men assembled together for a very long time. I'm proud to be one of them, even if, as we all are, very frightened at times. We believe we go in again to San Carlos Bay tomorrow night to start disembarking our passengers. Nobody, unless he, or she, is a fool, looks forward to it. The Argentinian Air Force still has a sting.

Despite those comments, he was not particularly impressed by the troops they had recently embarked:

> We are not as enamoured with our new passengers as with our friends of the RM Commando and 3 Para, who were our guests for seven weeks ... They now realise that we run a 'tight ship' in the interest of everybody's lives. That includes keeping the ship clean, which is as important now as ever. I have said enough on this subject for my and all our feelings to be understood ... The Guards are a funny lot and I still do not believe they are facing up to the realisation of tomorrow and the succeeding days, perhaps weeks. As somebody said today, if there are many officer casualties, Debrett's will have to be drastically revised.[8]

They successfully, and without incident, disembarked their latest passengers. He noted in his entry dated 3 June that:

> We have now achieved what is quite a feat and almost unbelievable – the landing, in effect, of the entire military force on the Falkland Islands. Quite remarkable and

---

[8] The Guards had come from a spell of public duty in London.

something to be very proud of.

Nearly a week later he noted:

> Coincidentally, *Military Incompetence* is the title of the book being read by our SNO. Unfortunately the last 48 hours has shown extraordinary incompetence or ill judgement among our own commanders.

He goes on to criticise the Argentinians equally, who:

> ... had not been too clever ... They could have caused much more havoc than they did and effectively prevented the landing of 3 Brigade and 5 Brigade. Thank God there has been incompetence on both sides.

The boredom of being in the 'holding box', doing nothing, as noted by other diarists, is noted here again:

> Morale is suffering a real hammering: this is our 10th week from Southampton and the eighth day in the TRALA [tug, repair and logistics area], with most the exciting action being the arrival of the odd helo. Not that we look for the unpleasant type of action, and hope and pray that it will not come our way.

After the surrender of the Argentinians and the cessation of hostilities ashore *Canberra* was:

> ... immediately dispatched to San Carlos Bay and thence to Port Stanley to collect POWs. 5000 on the first load and a further 5000 on the second leg. All right in theory, but where do we take them? ... The plight of these hapless individuals is appalling. Some 11,000 are held in the open on the airport runway in the most atrocious weather. Very cold, −18 °C wind chill factor at night with frequent rain or snow showers ... It really is a mercy mission

By 18 June:

> We are now a POW ship with some 4200 Argentinians on board ... Apart from the stench of peat and unwashed bodies (now all washed) the prisoners have been very little trouble. The great majority are only too delighted to be

warm, dry, well fed and on their way home.

They arrived at Puerto Madryn in Argentina 19 June. His entry for that day is given in full:

This must have been the most bizarre day of all our lives. We arrived at Puerto Madryn in Argentina at 13.30, having been escorted in from the twelve-mile territorial limit by an Argentina type 42 frigate who was polite, almost friendly and helpful! [The voice over the radio] spoke perfect English with an Oxford accent. Our 4167 prisoners were landed efficiently in record time with the utmost cooperation from the Argentines and we sailed for the Falklands again at 18.00. The weather was perfect, sunshine and cloudless blue skies but cold. The prisoners themselves, in the majority, said fond farewells to the ship's company and EMF [embarked military force], shaking their hands and even attempting on occasion to kiss them on the cheek in the Latin way. Something none of us present will ever forget and we all keep pinching ourselves that it really happened. The pilot was a nice little man, not very effective but friendly. It is hardly believable that a week ago we were killing each other. Now we are on our way back to Port Stanley to pick up other 3000 or so prisoners and repeat the trip. I do hope this is the end of this madness and we will shortly return to Southampton.

Three days later, on their return to Port Stanley, they received the good news that instead of returning to Argentina they were indeed to return to Southampton, taking with them the majority of 3 Brigade. He commented:

The feeling of elation in the ship does not need describing. It is the dream we have always had, to take back those that we brought out safely to Southampton. We rarely dared openly to express our hope but now that it is confirmed news we can, surely, be a little euphoric. What does surprise me is the petty bickering among the services.

All in their own way superb people but harbouring stupid jealousies such as arguing about what cabin each should occupy. Many other instances could be mentioned. It is not only a jealousy between the Navy, Army and Air Force, but between units within each. I do not understand it but it is childish. Almost always it is a case of communications, or lack of them through human stupidity, and if there has been one major failing in this war it has been in the communications field ... I must not be too critical as is it is intended more as a diary of events.

Despite the rigours that they had been through, the catering department had managed to husband the stores well, and he noted that:

Uganda is in the anchorage with us and Jeff Clark came over for lunch today. Rarely, I believe, has anybody gone to war as comfortably as we have, as I have recorded before, and lunchtime illustrates the point. The cold collation was started with caviar accompanied by Tio Pepe, followed by shrimps and cold meats with a Macon, rounded off with an excellent cheeseboard, coffee and port. It must be granted P&O go to war in style.[9]

They eventually sailed, having embarked over 2000 mainly Royal Marine commandos, including their brigadier Julian Thompson. They had been in communication with the Ministry of Defence about their destination, as Plymouth was the choice of the MoD. However, on 28 June:

We have finally won our desire to return to our home port of Southampton ... It is apparent that CG RM [Commandant General Royal Marines] and others in London/Northwood do not understand the feelings of all of us out here in the Task Force. The Brigadier finally clinched it with a signal ...

Once they had cleared the area of the Falklands they removed all the blackout and started to return the ship to her normal

---

[9] See also Uganda's dinner menu for 19 June.

state. Their return trip was not without incident. On 30 June they undertook a RAS with RFA *Appleleaf*, which took eight hours to transfer 2500 tons of fuel. He recorded:

> The meeting was not unalloyed joy, as their captain ..., quite unsolicited, ... called me on the bridge-to-bridge telephone and started a conversation: quote 'with all the money you have made out of the government, about £50 million, I would have thought you could have afforded a less tattered Blue Ensign.'

Their ETA was confirmed for Southampton on 11 July and he records that the return would be exciting, with many VIPs involved. By 3 July they were at Ascension Island, where they slowed down to receive some stores, their mail and some passengers. They also met up again with *Elk*, and when they overtook her again:

> She gave us a superb display with flares and a 21-gun salute. We replied with our GPMG [general purpose machine gun] and a flag salute.

His view of the Ministry of Defence was not so favourable:

> The war with various departments of MoD is worse than fighting the Argentines. The conflict with all the various interests is quite unbelievable. The only people who have a common purpose and any organisation are P&O.

Nor had his opinion of the press improved:

> The press still show they have little integrity and hound our lives and there is no doubt it will get worse with some 40+ invading us next Sunday morning. A press conference at 0715. Great days!

The next entry in Captain Scott-Masson's journal is dated 7 October, when he recorded the events of the arrival in Southampton on 11 July:

> It was a perfect summer's day ... Nothing went wrong – it could have been stage-set. The small craft surrounded and accompanied us from the Isle of Wight to the berth. For me, personally, it was memorable beyond my descriptive

powers ... The balloons, the cheers, the warmth, the pride, the honest excitement bring tears to the eyes as I write this three months later.

His return home brought other excitements:

The St Paul's thanksgiving service (a service arousing some controversy), being a guest at dinner of the prime minister, Margaret Thatcher, dinner as guest of Lord Inchcape, guest at the Cardiff Royal British Legion concert and many other engagements. Finally the award of a CBE in the Falklands Honours List was a great prize and I look forward to the visit to Buckingham Palace with Anne-Marie and the family in 1983. Mention must be made of wonderful support of Anne-Marie and so many others during this whole epic.

Uganda

The *Uganda* was built in Glasgow for the British India Steam Navigation Company to run on their London to East Africa service. Launched in January 1952, she ran together with the *Kenya* until changes in travel patterns caused by the increasing level of air passenger traffic caused regular liner services to become less and less economic. In 1967 she was converted to become a school ship, to join the *Nevasa*, which was already operating in that role. Her first passage after her extensive conversion was in February 1968. The conversion works included converting former cargo holds into dormitories and providing an assembly hall, cinemas, a games deck and swimming pools. At the same time a new re-equipped wheelhouse was constructed and additional lifeboats were provided. She became well established as a school ship, and in April 1982 was on a cruise in the Mediterranean with schoolchildren on board.

Because of the existence of a complete archive of the daily notices that were put out by the ship's office, under the heading 'Today's Arrangements', the daily orders issued by the naval party when they joined the ship in Gibraltar and the ship's voyage log, it has been possible to provide an account of life on board *Uganda* for that period from April until the first week in August when she returned to the UK.

On 11 April Captain Brian Biddick broadcast to the ship:

Good morning, ladies and gentlemen. Good morning, boys and girls. This is the captain speaking. I have to tell you that *Uganda* has been requisitioned by the government. I have been instructed to proceed direct to Naples, where the cruise will be terminated. Homeward flight details and travel arrangements are still being coordinated in London and I will promulgate this information when it is received on board. I expect to arrive in Naples at 4 p.m. on Tuesday 13 April and anticipate that disembarkation will take place shortly after. Both the company and all of us here in *Uganda* truly appreciate your disappointment, but the circumstances are beyond our control.

On the same day he issued a notice to the ship's company setting out the terms and conditions of service under government requisition. The terms were:

1. All officers and crew will be sailing on a voluntary basis in accordance with the recent agreement. Basic earnings will increase by 150 per cent when ... south of 7 degrees south.
2. Task – The ship will be serving as a hospital ship, fully declared under the Geneva Convention and properly marked as such. Although her role may require the ship to enter the risk area her declaration will offer the highest degree of protection.
3. Service discipline – Crew will be subject to normal disciplinary powers of the master of the ship.
4. Active service – In the very nature of the case, active service cannot be excluded, but will be declared, if at all, only if it appears to both flag officer commanding and the secretary of state that it is absolutely necessary.

Having read the above, please advise your head of department whether or not you are willing to continue serving in *Uganda* on a voluntary basis, after meeting with me in the restaurant at 5 p.m. this evening, when I will endeavour to answer any questions you may have with the information I have available at the moment. Please treat this information as STRICTLY CONFIDENTIAL. It is NOT to be disseminated to passengers.

From Naples, after having disembarked all the passengers, she proceeded to Gibraltar to be converted and repainted as a hospital ship. The works were completed in order for her to sail from there on Monday 19 April. She sailed in the morning, and in the afternoon had a practice RAS with RFA *Olna*. She then sailed south towards Freetown, through light winds with a steadily increasing temperature as they approached Sierra Leone.

A policy decision had been made on *Uganda* that as far as possible normal life would be continued and that the ship-board entertainment regime would continue. So on the day after they sailed there was evening entertainment in the music room, with a syndicate quiz, with background music at 10.30 p.m. The naval party of doctors and medical staff were provided with their own daily orders and information, and on that same day the first lieutenant of the naval party made the position of the Royal Navy on board very clear in the information that he provided:

While SS *Uganda* is under Royal Naval control it is intended to allow her staff to operate as a cruise ship until casualties arrive on board. This means that cruising watches will be established for medical guard duties and mealtimes, and recreation spaces and facilities will be controlled in a manner compatible with a passenger ship. Once casualties are received the Navy will begin to dictate the routines more stringently to ensure efficient care of patients.

In addition to the entertainment programme, religious services took place on virtually every day, for both Church of England and Roman Catholic faiths. On 22 April, for example, at 12.00 holy mass was held, and at 18.00 holy communion took place. The evening entertainment on that day was 'Give Us a Clue' (charades). These games were held in the music room. It was asked that 'any officer who uses the grand piano is requested to replace the leather cover after use.'

The captain, Brian Biddick, had become ill on the way to Freetown and was flown to the UK to hospital, but unfortunately died on 12 May. Captain Jeff Clark took over as master in his place.

They arrived at Freetown on 25 April and sailed later that same day. As the midday temperature alongside was over 33 °C and there was virtually no wind it was a welcome departure. The newsletter from the naval party commented 'when we were at Freetown, we all said it was the hottest weather we had ever experienced, so we were glad to set sail to sea again.' By 28 April they were at anchor off Ascension Island. On the way the Royal Marine band, who were embarked on board, gave a concert, and the ceremony to mark the crossing of the equator was held. On that evening the captain and officers of the *Uganda* hosted a cocktail party for the Royal Naval officers on board.

A particular problem on board was the small amount of fresh water that the ship carried. This was later to some extent mitigated when two desalination plants were installed on board. However, until that stage rigorous attempts to control the amount of fresh water being used were made, including virtually daily notices in the crew and naval party information sheets – for example on 29 April, at anchor at Ascension Island, the naval daily orders quoted:

> Captain Clark made a broadcast yesterday explaining the water situation. Our new station does not look a promising position to RAS water, so rationing has become an immediate necessity. To save water in the galley, lunchtime will become a cold cuts meal on a self-help basis, using disposable plates and cutlery.

Washing water was rationed. The ship's crew was advised that baths were not to be used and:

> Shower sparingly – turn water on – get wet – water off – soap – water on to rinse off soap. If you stand under the shower for 10 minutes, you will use all the fresh water in

about 10 days. We may have to be at sea for 30!

They received more water from the *Stena Seaspread* two days later, which enabled them to continue on their way south. On that evening, in the music room, was a ladies night and banquet dinner, followed by dancing. In the assembly hall a film was shown and there was also a quiz. By 4 May, not only was there still a severe and ongoing problem with the amount of water that was being consumed on board, but the amount of beer consumed was also giving cause for concern, and rationing was introduced to ensure that remaining stocks would last for a further 55 days.

On 7 May *Uganda* met a Royal Naval convoy led by HMS *Antrim* and undertook a RAS with RFA *Tidespring*, following which they set off for their operating position at maximum speed. As they approached their operating position, the hospital standing orders were issued, setting out the clear responsibilities and duties of the medical officer in charge and the master, in order that the ship could operate as a hospital ship as efficiently as possible. Among the details was noted:

> When the medical officer in charge and the master are in uniform and going aboard a man-of-war, the medical officer is to be considered the senior, and to take precedence. When boarding a merchant ship, including their hospital ship, the position of the master, as captain of the ship, should be recognised by allowing him to proceed aboard first. Constant liaison with the master, regarding major and minor hospital defects, is to be maintained. The master should frequently be invited to accompany the medical officer on his rounds of the hospital.

A further section of the standing orders gave instruction on foreign nationals, starting:

> Any foreign nationals received as casualties will be treated in compliance with the Geneva Convention 12 August 1949, in all respects as casualties of our own forces. The one exception is that a secure area may be designated and a guard posted to assist the medical staff.

One of the guards was armed.

Weekly newsletters were sent from the ship to the P&O head office for forwarding to the families of those on board. On 10 May the weekly newsletter noted, among other things:

> Entertainment continues at a fairly high level with committees formed to produce a programme of events. There is a good library on board supplemented by some 5000 paperbacks provided by the people of Gibraltar. The BBC World Service, including news about Britain, is still being received so we are well informed of world and home events.

On the next day they embarked the first casualties, which arrived by Sea King helicopter. The weather by this time had become less pleasant, with the temperature falling to 7 °C, and on 15 May the wind increased to a storm force 10, which made the ship roll up to 18 degrees to both port and starboard.

The next newsletter to head office in London included the following news:

> *Uganda* arrived in the holding position on Wednesday 12 May and on the same day our first few patients arrived by helicopter. The patients, naval ratings, were injured during the attack on HMS *Sheffield* and I am pleased to say they are recovering quite nicely. It was on this day that we received the sad news about Captain Biddick. To date we have had 69 helicopter landings, mainly in practice, and all the ship's company are now well into the routine of receiving planes. Since arriving at our holding position (known as the 'NOSH box' – naval ocean going surgical hospital) we have met up with one of the other hospital ships – the converted survey ship, the HMS *Hecla* of 3500 tons – and she is keeping near to us. *Hecla* is known on board as our 'chicken', *Uganda* (16,900 tons) being the 'mother hen'. Other ships call us 'Nurse *Uganda*'.

On 24 May they were ordered to go from their holding position, the 'NOSH box', to Middle Bay, which is at the entrance to Falkland Sound. The voyage log notes, succinctly:

21.30 Entered Middle Bay, surprised HMS *Coventry*.

They stayed there for the rest of the week, receiving helicopters with casualties during that time. The *Uganda* was not the only hospital ship in the area, as an Argentine hospital ship, the *Bahia Paraiso*, was also receiving casualties, but from the Argentinian army. On 4 June *Uganda*, having moved out of Falkland Sound into the Red Cross box holding area, transferred Argentinian casualties to her by helicopter. The P&O newsletter dated 10 June described the encounter in detail:

> We rendezvoused with the Argentinian hospital ship *Bahia Paraiso*, a modern ship, some 10,000 tons, and carrying her own Puma helicopter. Medical inspection teams from both ships were exchanged and Argentinian patients transferred to the *Bahia Paraiso*. The staff of the *Bahia Paraiso* could not have been more cooperative, offering us both medical and food stores – even wine! Small gifts were passed between ships – it was good to know that a friendly rapport exists between the hospital ships.

Further casualties were transferred and there was more contact between the two ships from time to time.

By this time the desalination plants were on board and the first, nicknamed Niagara, had been set to work but had still not refilled the tanks. A note to the crew on 25 May said 'Save water – have a dirty weekend.'

On 26 May the weekly newsletter to head office commented:

> This week has been fairly active on the operational aspect rather than the medical. We first met up with one of our tugs and sent across to her our chief radio officer and third radio officer to repair the radio. This was done most successfully. The following day we received our desalination plant ... It arrived in 20 separate lifts by helicopter with a technician to help put all the bits together. It is now producing good fresh water – much to everyone's amazement – the engineering staff and all concerned have worked wonders ... The next day one more of our chickens hatched in the shape of another

hospital ship, the sister ship to the previous one, so we now have two chickens [*Hecla* and *Hydra*] accompanying us.

A collection had been made on board in memory of Captain Biddick, and on 27 May Captain Clark, in the daily notices, acknowledged the £288.75 donated on behalf of Captain Biddick's family.

Among the items in the newsgram sent by the naval party to their families, it was noted:

> Our naval nurses have adapted admirably to shipboard life. It is the first time that QARNNS [Queen Alexandra's Royal Naval Nursing Service] ratings have been to sea, although QARNNS sisters were embarked in hospital ships during and after the Second World War. We have seen both the islands and enemy aircraft.

The ship received a message from Surgeon Commander Rick Jolly, who was the officer commanding the medical squadron of the Royal Marines, at the beginning of June:

> Ladies and gentlemen, I want to thank you, on behalf of the group of 90 officers and men running the medical and surgical facilities ashore, for everything you've done for us. You will have heard that conditions are primitive – they are, and blood mixes poorly with dirt. However we all know that our efforts have not been wasted when the medevac helicopter lifts off each morning. Our proud boast is that everyone who has made it to Ajax Bay alive has also got to you in the same way, is only possible because of your support.
>
> Yesterday was quiet from the air attack point of view; hopefully today will be the same as we are burying the dead of the Second Battalion, the Parachute Regiment – four officers, including the CO, and 13 men. You may have heard also about the two unexploded bombs in our building. They are only 150 feet and 3 walls away from the operating tables. The RAF bomb disposal experts say that, now 36 hours have passed, they are unlikely to explode

because of a time delay fuse!! Even so we won't let them defuse the bombs because we haven't got anywhere else to go. When the air-raid warning is given all the staff don tin hats and carry on working. The bombs have forced us into the far end of our building, about 30 per cent of the original space, and that's another reason why we need you and depend on you.

We are also expecting 1200 prisoners today, including about 40 lightly wounded. They will be put on one of the ships. The prisoners so far have been cold, underfed and frightened but as soldiers they have fought well. The determination and bravery of the Air Force pilots is widely admired, even by us, the ground troops they are attacking. It is possible to respect their courage while cheering loudly as a Rapier or Seawolf converts the Mirages and Skyhawks into their component parts. Once again, thanks for everything. We owe you a lot. Best wishes also to our former customers – hope you're enjoying the sea views!

They received a further message from Surgeon Commander Jolly, particularly for those casualties on board who were from 2nd Battalion Parachute Regiment:

We buried your colleagues on the small hill above the hospital on Sunday afternoon. Over 100 men watched in silence and brilliant sunshine as one by one the bodies of 17 fallen comrades were carried down into the grave. Each body bag was covered with the union flag, carried by six men of similar rank. Colonel H's body was preceded by the 2 i/c and carried by the company commanders. Each body was then saluted in silence and respect – 15 paras, including a sapper corporal; a Marine and Royal Marine officer helicopter pilot who was shot down going to pick up H as a 'casevac'. You'll all be glad to hear that Ajax Bay's track record as a medical and surgical facility continues to be 100 per cent. Yesterday saw the 100th operation under general anaesthetic. The total is now 107 out of 260 admissions. We send our best to all our customers. More news later once again ... Thanks for everything.

From the beginning of June, when they had over 130 casualties on board, until the 20th *Uganda* spent the daylight hours in Grantham Sound, off Falkland Sound, receiving casualties by helicopter, sailing out to the Red Cross box overnight. The captain described the view in Grantham Sound:

> It was good to see land all around us and to lie quietly at anchor. The vista is much like the Scottish Highlands, with snow on the hills and even Aberdeen Angus grazing on the cliffs. Some people, presumably from San Carlos, came onto the hilltops to gaze at the Hospital Ship *Uganda*.

In the daily newsletter on 9 June, the medical officer in charge wrote:

> The ship now functions as a fully integrated hospital unit. The success of the hospital's role is due, in no small part, to the unfailing support of the P&O crew members who turn out regularly for casualty reception and stretcher-bearing duties. The unseen supporting role of other crew members; the many and varied duties of the Royal Marines Band personnel; the RN Medical Branch staff and others are all part of the success which benefits the patients who depend on us. Thank you.

It was as well that they were such an efficient unit, because that day was the busiest they had experienced. The newsletter explained:

> This day was the busiest we have had up to date, following the attack on the ships *Sir Galahad* and *Sir Tristram*. We received a large number of casualties and at one stage a helicopter was arriving every 10 minutes. Volunteers were called for to assist in casualty reception for both walking wounded and stretcher cases, thus relieving the hard-pressed medical staff. The assistance, which came from all departments, was an excellent response. When night came we were back outside into our holding area.

They received news of the surrender of Port Stanley on 14 June, and within three days had received congratulatory messages from the Ministry of Defence and P&O. The menu for dinner in the officers' mess on 19 June would appear to indicate something of a celebration, as it offered:

Smoked salmon
Asparagus tips vinaigrette
Cream of tomato soup consommé royale
Fillet of sole bonne femme
Tournedos Rossini
Creamed and French fried potatoes
Peas flamande, cauliflower
Assorted cold cuts
Salad
Mayonnaise
Coupe Alaska
Cheese and biscuits
Fresh and dried fruit
After dinner mints
Tea, coffee

This could be accompanied by house wines or by the recommended wines of the day which were Macon Rouge or Berich Bernkastel Riesling Langenbach.

Two days later, after a RAS with the RFA *Olna*, *Uganda* moved into Port William and anchored in the inner harbour, close to Port Stanley. They were at anchor there for a week before sailing for the Red Cross box, to rendezvous with HMS *Hecla* to transfer stores and personnel. However, the increasing wind prevented that and on 30 June the voyage log records that the wind was gusting force 11 – almost hurricane force. They spent the day steaming in the shelter of East Falkland. During that evening the ship celebrated a 'South Atlantic New Year', complete with an address to the haggis by the ship's chief engineer, followed by a ceilidh. The weather eased the next day, 1 July, and they were able to re-enter Port William and anchor in the inner harbour once more. They then received the news that Headquarters Land Forces Falkland Islands had agreed that short periods of shore leave in small groups could be granted, for an hour's duration. The conditions for shore leave included the note that hotels and public houses were out of bounds and that the officer in charge of each party was provided with a map to indicate where they could and could not go.

The voyage log indicated that next day they sailed back out to sea for a 'round Falklands cruise' – in fact, in order to make water from the two desalination plants. The weather was not conducive to a 'cruise', as thick snow was falling, the temperature was around 0 °C at midday for the next two days and a full gale was blowing, which made any proposed landings impracticable. Before they had returned to Port William they had reached the furthest west and furthest southerly points of their deployment.

While on their cruise they received a telex from P&O London containing an extract from a letter written by Admiral Sir John Fieldhouse, who said, 'I cannot say too often or too clearly how important has been the Merchant Navy's contribution to our efforts. Without the ships taken up from trade, the operation could not have been undertaken and I hope this message is clearly understood by the British nation.'

Back in their anchorage in Port William, they held a children's party for some 92 children. This started at about 12.30, and the children were treated to music from the Marine Band, party games, lunch, and a cartoon show before being handed goody bags and returned ashore at 3.30. The next day the question was asked by the ship's entertainment officer, 'Who had the most fun, the children or the ship's company?'

The voyage log noted on 13 July that '*Uganda* ceases to be a hospital ship.' News was received of her future programme and likely sailing date. The future programme included embarking a total of 640 Gurkhas, with their kit, stores and appropriate rations, if available, and, following their embarkation and having received the stores, to sail for Ascension Island and then the UK. They received a signal from C in C Fleet on that day which said:

On the occasion of your metamorphosis you can justly feel proud of the outstanding success of your role as principal hospital ship in support of the Falklands Task Force.

Uganda will long be remembered by all who benefited from your skill and care. BZ [naval code for 'very well done']

On the next evening, en route from the anchorage in Port William to Grantham Sound, a ship's company dance was held, with disco dancing from 9 p.m. until 1 a.m. next morning. At 8 a.m. on that same morning they anchored to embark 320 Gurkhas, moving to Fox Bay overnight to embark another 237. The embarkation was carried out by Chinook helicopter, and also by the ship's lifeboats.

After completing watering from the *Fort Toronto* and taking on stores they sailed from Port William before midday, steaming out into a force 8 gale. Two days later, on 21 July, the voyage log notes, 'rendezvous with *Dumbarton Castle*. Transfer of mail and pot noodles by boat.' As the wind for the past three days had been gale force 8 and was still force 6 on the 21st, a boat transfer in the Southern Ocean in those conditions would have been quite exciting. It is not possible to determine whether the pot noodles were transferred from *Uganda* or from the *Dumbarton Castle*, although the former is rather more likely.

In the following days the weather improved, the temperature went up and the wind decreased. By the time that they arrived off Ascension Island on 28 July temperature was over 26 °C. Allotted sunbathing areas, divided into spaces for officers, female officers and ratings, naval ratings, troops and P&O crew were made. With over 1100 people on board, this was necessary to ensure the best use of space.

The naval daily orders on 23 July included the statistics of the number of helicopter landings that had been undertaken, up to when they sailed for the UK. A total of 1043 landings were made and over 3000 personnel transported to and from *Uganda* by helicopter. Of those, 21 were by Argentinian helicopters. As the days progressed other reports were completed, including one by the matron, who made the following comments about the *Uganda*'s crew:

P&O personnel gave great help with patients. They acted as stretcher bearers, patient handlers, porters and took patients from triage to wards. They helped in the wards, appearing regularly to feed patients, give out drinks, bed bathing and doing tasks they were not trained for and were of great help and assistance. The service given by P&O was excellent, providing a good laundry, ward cleaning and meals service. Food was brought to the wards in heated boxes, drinks were dispensed by the stewards. Hot snacks were available in the dining room for the staff going on and off duty in the middle of the night. Mealtimes in the main dining room were adjusted to suit the needs of watch keepers. Cleaning materials, toilet soap, gash bags etc. were supplied by P&O as were washing bowls, pedal bins etc.

They were at Ascension Island for only a few hours, taking on fuel and water and transferring some stores and personnel. They crossed the equator on 30 July and on the next day the captain issued a notice giving details of their arrival in Southampton. The captain, all the officers and the European crew were to be relieved on their arrival. On the day before they entered the Bay of Biscay *Uganda* was overflown by a Sea King helicopter and two Sea Harriers, which it was presumed were from HMS *Illustrious.*

They entered the English Channel on Sunday 8 August, and 24 hours later the pilot embarked off the Needles, Isle of Wight, to take her to Southampton Water, securing alongside in Southampton docks at 11.00. From leaving Gibraltar to returning to Southampton they had steamed 22,709 nautical miles, had admitted 730 casualties (of which 159 were Argentinian) and carried out 903 surgical operations. They had also served 212,343 meals, which had taken, among other things, 30,000 pounds of flour, 108,000 eggs, 2000 gallons of milk, 40,000 pounds of meat, 17 tons of potatoes and 7 tons of ice cream. Nine thousand loaves and 144,000 rolls had been baked.

As with other ships, they were met by parties from the ship's owners, P&O, including the deputy chairman and managing director, the press and VIPs. After the welcoming party and all the crew and officers had left ship, the *Uganda* then proceeded to the River Tyne for a refit, before re-entering service.

In January 1983 she was chartered again by the Ministry of Defence to become a troopship, running between Ascension Island and Port Stanley, and she continued in this role for nearly two years, but was then retired and laid up in the River Fal, before being sold for scrap.

Canberra and *Uganda*

The general manager's tale

Maurice Onslow had initially hoped to go to sea as a deck officer, but he was prevented by eyesight problems, so after completing national service and accountancy training, he joined Orient Line as an assistant purser. As Orient Line became part of P&O the number of passenger ships in the merged company increased. He stayed with the company as it grew and changed in various ways, including becoming an operator of ferry services. By 1982 he had come ashore, after sailing as chief purser, and was the general manager of P&O Hotel Services Department, in overall charge of the catering and purser's departments for the entire fleet. As such, when the *Canberra* and *Uganda* were taken up from trade, he was heavily involved. He takes up the story, which he dictated:

> On Saturday 3 April I was called to go into the office and told that, under secrecy, the *Canberra* was going to be taken up but this wasn't to be told to anybody until Margaret Thatcher had made an announcement in the House of Commons. At that time she was between Naples and Gibraltar, on the homeward voyage.
>
> I had to look at the re-manning of it, particularly because the Indian government didn't want the Indian crew to go into the war zone. I also had to look at re-storing. I had to look at the obvious things, for example if there were going to be limited [meal] services. I assumed, which turned out to be correct, that officers and senior

NCOs were going to be in the forward restaurant and junior NCOs and the ratings were all aft ... *Canberra*, at that time, offered a wonderful service, because at the after end of the restaurant there were two double doors ... which meant that you could get people coming in and going out, so that was of great assistance. If it was going to be done that way, I went to what I had seen on the *Uganda*, which were steel trays with compartments. It means that you can only put a certain amount [of food] on at any given time. At the forward end it would be waiter service, whereas you didn't need any people in the after end and then they produced their own people to clear up, so that was a real, major point ... I decided that that would be the best way to do it.

Then I went into the food side. I re-manned it completely and then had to talk to another department, the personnel department. I had to go to the pool because a lot of people, like the deck crew, who were Indian, had to be replaced from the pool. There were then a number of people from the pool in the hotel department. It wasn't as bad as *Uganda*, which had to be totally pool because she had a Muslim, Calcutta, crew. So I sorted it out as to what I thought was the right way to provide service for the feeding and then went into thinking about how to work out what the quantities would be so I had visitations here [in Southampton] and subsequently on the phone to Bath. They wouldn't say. They referred to everything in man days and it's not what we did, we called them victualling days, which is a different way of looking at it, and they wouldn't tell me how many people there were going to be. I couldn't work out how it was going to operate until Mr [Lieutenant Commander] Muxworthy arrived. We discussed possible menus ... although by that time the decision had been made as far as the differing services in the aft and forward restaurants were concerned. I then came home here with my trusted calculator, which I still have upstairs, to work out some figures.

There were some problems with storing. She had limited refrigerator space. She could do a world cruise with a top-up in Australia and New Zealand, but to go for an unknown length of time you had to fill the store rooms up. She had a further problem with the limited amount of water she could carry and a problem with frozen things, so you had to go to tinned, which was the route that I wanted to go down. Then, on the Monday, I was allowed to speak to my immediate staff about what was happening and for them to fully agree how realistic my theories were, which they all did.

Then we started storing *Canberra* as soon as she came in, but in the meantime I had spoken to the purser and said we don't know how many people we are going to be carrying. When *Canberra* was introduced into service she carried 2200 and then that was reduced to 1600/1700. The reason for that was that the upper bunks at the after end of the ship had been folded up out of the way, so I wanted them to check to see if there were mattresses in all of them. It was just one of those things, so we were able to find another 600 berths very easily.

We were storing busily and then we were given the details of timing and we were allowed an extra 24 hours. The suppliers here really came up trumps and the dockers as well at that time, although there were all sorts of problems in the docks. In the process of it we filled the storerooms, freezers and chillers, filled the dry stores, and the only way to do it then was to put tinned goods from the two entrances on D Deck, all the way across the foyer, up to the next deck. By then I was getting into panic state, not from Martin [chief officer] but from the gentleman from what at that time was called Three Quays, who was panic-stricken that we were loading so much that she was going down to her marks, but I was saying 'look at all those containers you are putting up there – you're putting on top weight but I'm putting in bottom weight.'[10] Then we decided that in the various bars we would floor them out with tinned goods, beer and minerals two deep on the floors of the bars, so the barman could just stand on them and serve. We had draught beer to start but then it would just be canned.

Then the ship sailed, and it was very emotional, and then Howard Langley said to me 'tomorrow *Uganda*?' And I came home and the next morning I was phoned to say can you go to Gibraltar to deal with the *Uganda*, she is being taken up – so she had to be re-manned and re-stored. I flew to Morocco – well, I flew to Gibraltar, but was diverted to Morocco. When I got to Gibraltar I was told that the crew didn't want to sail because they were going to a war zone. It took a lot of discussion and influence from the deputy purser and what was called the butler [the Indian head steward] to convince the crew ... I had to stand up and say that she is protected under the Geneva Convention. Fortunately Marika [Maurice's wife] used to work for Red Cross and she had a book which I could quote from, as to what they can't do if you have a Red Cross, so I said, 'look over the side – you can see that the ship is being painted with a Red Cross.'

Then the next real problem was that the Navy had cleared out a large part of the victualling stores at Gibraltar and had taken it all away, so there was only a limited amount available. Because *Uganda* had altered course, she had originally been going into Naples[11] and there were to have been two containers from the UK there including one that had MK [Muslim killed] mutton in, because it was a Calcutta Muslim crew. I tried Gibraltar without luck,

---

[10] The stability of the ship is of crucial importance, and the loading of stores would have a significant effect.

[11] She did call at Naples, but only long enough to discharge the schoolchildren who had been on an educational cruise.

because the border with Spain was closed then. I then tried in Morocco. No good. Tried Tunisia through agents there. No good. Morocco had been the obvious place because there was a ferry service across ... Of course the Muslim crew would not have sailed if they thought they had not got enough MK mutton on board, so I had to approach the admiral's office and fortunately there was a gentleman there who had been on a secondment with P&O ... I explained the problem and I was then told they would think about it ... In the end we had a lorry of frozen MK mutton and other items loaded on the back end of a Hercules at RAF Lyneham and sent out. It was going to Ascension but it called in at Gibraltar where we were waiting with lorries to load it and take it down to the ship and then she sailed. There were some very tense moments. I was so glad after a fortnight or so to get home but then had a phone call from a person in MoD asking me about various aspects. I blew my top and said if you don't mind, I have just been working for 24 hours, so it seemed, non-stop ...

When the ships came back I found it extraordinary because we kept getting calls to go up to the MoD and we ended up in several meetings where they were all sitting round the table ... It was getting annoying because ... in the case of the *Canberra*, there was a suggestion that the Mayor of Plymouth ... had said that the ship should return to Plymouth because that was where 42 Commando was based. We got a message, which I think was from Admiral Woodward, saying that the ship started from Southampton, it is her home port and she will go back there. It was just as well because of her draft – if she had had to go over the Hamoaze [in Plymouth Sound] she would have grounded.

But the next one was when the *Uganda* came back. That all went reasonably well, although we did get locked into the MoD [on one occasion] because of the pass system. You had to get a chit signed and then go from one person to the other, and the place was dead at six o'clock at night. When the *Uganda* came in she landed up at Newcastle, at Smith's Dock. I joined her up there and then we came back down here. After only a few voyages back as a school ship again the Navy decided that they wanted a ship to go backwards and forwards from Ascension to the Falklands and it seemed to suit them to have her. They wanted her to be restored to Navy standards, to have a flight deck put on her again and then all the RAS equipment which would have gone through the school room, so the technical people came along and then Malta docks said they couldn't do it so we came back, having been to this meeting with all these FCO [Foreign and Commonwealth Office] people and other pontifical types at which the person in charge of the meeting had said what about Naples? Objection – you know the Italians, friends of Galtieri. The French – ah, you know the French. They went round to Spain – no, definitely not, General Galtieri's home ground. Gibraltar – no, we have already been there. How about Portugal? Suddenly this bloke woke up, he had been half asleep, and said ah, our oldest ally. She ended up in Falmouth and did sterling service for two years from Ascension to Port Stanley.

3

The container ships

Atlantic Conveyor

Atlantic Causeway

Atlantic Conveyor

Owned by the Cunard Steam Ship Company, *Atlantic Conveyor* was an 18,000 ton specialist container and roll-on/roll-off cargo ship built in 1969, and she was designed, as her name implies, for transatlantic duties. Containers were stored on her upper deck and she had six lower decks joined by ramps. The main deck opened onto a stern ramp, designed to be lowered to an appropriately designed jetty. She had a cruising speed of 22 knots from steam turbine engines driving the twin propellers. Although by today's standards she was relatively small, 30 years ago she was equivalent in size to the aircraft carriers HMS *Hermes* and HMS *Invincible*, being slightly over 200 metres long, and she could carry as many aircraft, after conversion, as either of the two 'real' aircraft carriers.

Although her upper deck was flat, all the obstructions for the securing of the containers had to be removed. The deck was painted with non-skid paint and had flight-deck markings applied. The clear deck area enabled her to transport 25 aircraft, including Chinook helicopters, Harrier jets and other helicopters.

Her normal crew was just 34, but they were augmented by a naval party of about 100. Existing accommodation was altered to provide more bunks, and two Portakabins were also installed on the upper deck, which accommodated 24 people. The works of conversion and taking on the stores took just 9 days. She then sailed from Plymouth with a partial load of aircraft, embarking 14 Harriers at Ascension Island.

The senior naval officer's tale

Captain Michael Layard, now Admiral Sir Michael Layard and a former Second Sea Lord, was appointed to the *Atlantic Conveyor* as senior naval officer in mid-April 1982. He wrote his 'Recollections of the Falklands Campaign by the Senior Naval Officer, SS *Atlantic Conveyor*' a month after the conflict finished. In this first excerpt from his recollections, he describes his first encounter with *Atlantic Conveyor* and her master, Captain Ian

North: [1]

> The next day I went to Liverpool, saw the ship and met her master, Ian North. Within 5 minutes of our meeting, I blessed my lucky stars for here, quite clearly, was a man in a million – short, squat and with a snowy, bushy beard, he was the very archetype of the Merchant Navy skipper, exuding energy, confidence and 'can do'.

After the conversion, they sailed on schedule. The recollections continue:

> On the evening of 25 April, just nine days after arriving in Devonport, we weighed anchor and after quickly testing out our RAS system with RFA *Grey Rover* set off to the South Atlantic in company with *Europic Ferry* ... With two captains on board, Ian North and I needed to be sure of our terms of reference – so we wrote them ourselves. He was plainly in command of his ship and responsible for its safety. However, when it came to our warlike functions it was my task to make sure that *Atlantic Conveyor* could react correctly. In essence I was in tactical command and the best analogy of our working relationship was as between admiral and captain. I told him what needed to be done and he, despite the strangeness of some of my directives, invariably did them. To the credit of this remarkable and talented old sea dog, he only blenched at one of my suggestions later on, which was to expedite a change of formation in the Task Group by taking a beeline through it; he preferred, not unnaturally, the roundabout route.[2]

> The *Atlantic Conveyor*'s senior officers all shared their accommodation with the naval party. Ian North, the chief officer John Brocklehurst and chief engineer Jimmy

---

[1] Some extracts from Michael Layard's account were published in J Winton, *Signals from the Falklands*, London, 1995.

[2] Taking his ship through the middle of a convoy of other ships would be any master's worst nightmare, not unlike pushing a pram across a motorway at rush hour.

Stewart all generously offered their day cabins as sleeping quarters for the squadron commanders and their senior officers. David Baston, CO 848, and Tim Gage, CO 809, were Ian North's guests and quickly became firm friends. Ian was 'Father' to everyone and went out of his way to get to know all my team. Many were the times I saw him on bridge wing or upper deck holding court to a spellbound group of young men. His stories were numerous and fascinating, his manner charming, and in very little time he was loved and revered throughout the ship ... We arrived [at Ascension Island] in the rain on 5 May to find the amphibious force already there: HMS *Fearless*, HMS *Intrepid*, *Canberra*, *Elk*, *Norland*, *Fort Toronto*, *Europic Ferry*, RFA *Stromness*, two RFA tankers and the LSLs ... If ever the adage 'we couldn't have done it without the Merchant Navy' came home to me it was at Ascension Island with my first glimpse of these soon to be famous ships.

The requirements of the task included the necessity for replenishment at sea (RAS), with parts of the Merchant Navy and Royal Navy sections of the crew joining in. The recollections continue:

The RAS party was a marvellous example of RN/MN cooperation. A scratch team of enthusiastic amateurs under the leadership of my capable fleet chief seaman, Mick Legg, and ably assisted by the ship's bosun John Dobson, was soon buttoning up the hoses quickly and professionally and eventually even doing it at night. The tanker, usually RFA *Tidepool*, kindly formed up on us, as Ian North was not happy that *Atlantic Conveyor*'s engines were responsive enough to do it the normal way ... On 19 May we joined the Task Group and took up station beside *Hermes* to transfer her ration of ten Harriers. The weather and sea state for this operation had worried me because a VTOL [vertical take-off and landing] aircraft is susceptible to an alarming loss of control if there is turbulence or deck movements when taking off vertically. Mercifully the sea was gentle and wind light for the transfer and nine of the ten launched uneventfully. The tenth pilot gave us and himself a fright when he tried to take off vertically but with his jet nozzles facing aft instead of down. He charged across the deck at the guardrails 20 feet away but retrieved the situation by slamming his nozzles to the vertical and leaping into the air just in time. Ian North turned to me with a twinkle in his eye and said, 'That's a novel way of doing it.'

On 25 May the invaluable work of the *Atlantic Conveyor* was tragically brought to an end by Exocet missiles, fired from Super Étendard jet fighters who believed their target was one of the aircraft carriers. In one sense it was, but not the carriers that the Argentinians assumed to be the echo on their radars.

Michael Layard's recollections continue:

'Air raid warning red – emergency stations, emergency stations.' I heard the broadcast on my way to the bridge and took the stairs three at a time as I pulled my life jacket over my head. I arrived to find that *Atlantic Conveyor* was in a turn to port, as ordered. I asked for a threat direction but none had been passed. Then, as the ship's head passed through east we felt and heard a loud explosion from aft. It wasn't long before the quantities of billowing acrid black smoke pointed at the likelihood of Exocet and on the bridge we started to try to establish the extent of the damage and casualty list. Reports began to filter through that the missile (or two as it transpired) had come into the port quarter 8 to 10 feet above the waterline ...

Only 20 minutes after being hit, it was clear that our ship was doomed and that all our attempts to quell the fires by activating the sprinkler systems, by carbon dioxide drenching, by shutting down the fan vents and by pumping hoses to every access into cargo decks, were to no avail. Already the whole of the upper deck was becoming too hot to stand on, despite drenching with fire hoses. Night was drawing in and the sea state beginning to worsen. Added to which I knew the fire was creeping forward and would reach thousands of gallons of kerosene and cluster bombs which could blow us to pieces at any moment.

Captain North and I both reached the conclusion to abandon ship together. The decision was a dreadful one for a master to make but Ian's calm and good sense prevailed ... By now conditions aft were decidedly unpleasant and it was high time that the command team ... took steps to abandon our stricken ship. Ian North was the last to leave and as I climbed down just below him the picture was crystal clear in my mind. I remember that the ship's side was literally glowing red in places and the paint peeling off in others. The descent seemed interminable, the more so as pieces of shrapnel from the explosions inside the ship were coming out through the side and singing past my ears. Added to which I was half expecting that she and I would blow up at any second.

I felt a quite unwarranted sense of relief as I dropped the last 10 feet into the water but this was very short-lived as I soon discovered while waiting for Ian North to join me. The climb down the ship's side had taken its toll on Ian for he was no chicken nor greyhound. After he had dropped into the icy sea beside me I held him up as he seemed to be floating rather lower in the water than was good for him and I then realised that our troubles had only just begun for it appeared that *Atlantic Conveyor* aimed to take us to the bottom with her ... Ian and I rode a couple of duckings and buffetings but time was running out and it was high time we got to a raft. My last sight of that dear old friend was as I gave him a strong shove in the small of the back for the nearest life raft. I then went under again, thought my number was really up this time and when, after what seemed a lifetime, I broke the surface again the scene was quite different. There was no sign of Ian North, merely an empty life raft and someone else floating face down beside me ...

We were superbly cared for by our rescue ships. I have an indelible memory as I walked dripping and frozen into the compartment where my fellow survivors were in *Alacrity*. A sea of shivering grey faces greeted me. Relief was the main emotion, tinged by anxiety as people searched for friends. Twelve of our number were dead or missing, including our beloved Ian North.

Michael Layard's last comments reflect on the nature of the transformation of the *Atlantic Conveyor* and what she had accomplished:

We called her the '30 Day Wonder', because from sailing to sinking that was the length of her operational life. And when they were gone, she and her incomparable old skipper, there was an ache in the hearts of all who had been part of *Atlantic Conveyor*'s astonishing metamorphosis ... With an 8000-mile logistic chain, Operation Corporate was a very close thing and there is no doubt that we could not have succeeded without the enormous contribution of our superb merchant service: ships and people.

The engineer's tale

Charles Drought, who was appointed to the *Atlantic Conveyor* for her Falklands deployment, published his memoirs of that time some 20 years after the event.[3] He had written a journal whilst he was still at sea, for the benefit of his family. The later publication of the book came as a result of showing his journal to a friend who recognised that it should have a wider audience. There is space here for no more than a brief summary of his experiences.

By 1982 he was a very experienced marine engineer, having already been at sea for 23 years. He was appointed senior third

---

[3] C Drought. NP 1840: the Loss of the Atlantic Conveyor. Birkenhead, 2003.

engineer and joined the ship in Liverpool, for her trip to Devonport to be converted. She sailed on 16 April, arriving in Devonport on the next day. He commented that 'the following morning all hell broke loose, dockyard workers swarmed like ants all over the ship.' He soon discovered that she was being converted for use as an aircraft carrier. But his main concern, as third engineer, was being able to supply enough fresh water for the additional crew they were to carry. He was able to telephone his wife just before they sailed on 26 April, but was not able to tell her very much, as the crew were under conditions of restriction of information; all letters that were sent at that time were under censorship.

They anchored in Plymouth Sound to test the fore and aft flight decks. Although they were carrying military stores below decks as well as aircraft on the upper deck, he was very worried that no defensive armament had been fitted to the ship. In the days after they sailed, the naval party and the regular crew settled into a combined routine for various lifeboat and emergency drills and learnt the new skills of replenishment at sea. He describes his dislike of the decision to call at Freetown on the trip to Ascension Island, to take on bunkers (engine fuel). This dislike was based on the construction of the *Atlantic Conveyor* for transatlantic duties: she was therefore not equipped with the appropriate engine-room ventilation for tropical waters. However, they were only in Freetown for one day, sailing on 2 May for Ascension Island.

When they crossed to the south of latitude 6 degrees south the Merchant Navy crew's pay increased by 150 per cent, on account of the war bonus which had been agreed. He made little of this, although the naval party were 'a little aggrieved at this bonanza to the crew'. They arrived at Ascension Island on 4 May to find the Task Force had arrived. The size of the fleet of Royal Navy and merchant ships caused him to go to his cabin 'deep in [his] own morbid thoughts'. The next day they sailed as part of the Assault Group, with *Canberra* to starboard and *Elk* to port. He had apparently got over his morbid thoughts, as he described it as 'a most impressive sight' and was 'moved at the sight of this armada'.

He describes the feelings on board at the news of the attack on HMS *Sheffield* on 4 May and the resulting loss of life. 'Since the sinking of the *Sheffield* it was all so different, something out of the ordinary, something they had never experienced before in their lives, the prospect that they could die a violent death'. His apprehension was increased when all the crew had to take a blood test in case of a transfusion being needed if they were wounded in action.

The Assault Group joined the Task Force on 18 May. On the next day, as described by Michael Layard above, the Harriers and some of the helicopters were transferred to HMS *Hermes*. Two days after the first landings the *Atlantic Conveyor* and the *Elk* were to have entered Falkland Sound – but events in the interim meant that although *Canberra*, *Norland* and the *Europic Ferry* had all gone into San Carlos to disembark troops and safely returned to the open sea, *Atlantic Conveyor* had stayed outside. On 25 May orders were received to enter Falkland Sound later that day. Charles Drought had been on watch from 1000 until 1400, and was asleep when 'action stations' was called. This was immediately followed by a heavy explosion; he remembered 'the whole of the *Conveyor* shuddered, and [I] fell flat on [my] face'. Recovering himself, although wet from water in a bucket which had been thrown from his bathroom and which had contained his dirty washing, he started on his way to his emergency station in the engine room. At that point a second explosion caused the ship to shudder and list more heavily to starboard. Following this he continued his descent to the engine room, noting as he did that those mustered at the emergency point in the officers' lounge were all in their survival suits. On his arrival in the control room he found that the glass in all the control gauges had been broken and was crunching under his feet. Conditions worsened rapidly. A third explosion confirmed the engineer's fears that all efforts to keep the ship afloat were not succeeding. The fires in the cargo decks were growing and advancing towards the cluster bombs and kerosene storage in the forward part.

'Abandon ship' was called, and the crew, including Charles Drought, had to climb down the rope ladders to the life rafts, which were already inflated in the water. He was fortunate in that, although falling the last few feet, he landed in a life raft and not in the sea. HMS *Alacrity* rescued survivors from the life rafts, coming close alongside to do so, firing lines over the life rafts to help pull them to a safe distance. After receiving excellent care from her crew, they were transferred by helicopter to the *British Tay*. Charles Drought was told subsequently that the co-pilot on the Sea King helicopter was none other than HRH Prince Andrew. The helicopter trip was not an experience that he enjoyed – and the descent onto the deck of the *British Tay* was even less pleasant. The trip ended on 5 June when she anchored off Ascension Island. After a second helicopter trip, from the ship to the shore, which he did not enjoy any more than the first, the survivors were flown by RAF VC10 aircraft to Brize Norton.

As a postscript, Charles Drought returned to sea, serving on Cunard container ships until retirement in July 1996, having spent 37 years at sea.

After the crew abandoned the *Atlantic Conveyor*, she was approached by the tug *Irishman* on 27 May. By that time she was still smouldering, listing to starboard and down by the stern. It had been considered of great importance to attempt to recover her because of the equipment she was carrying. The *Irishman* managed to pass a line, after some of her crew had boarded. A towing line was connected, those of the *Irishman*'s crew that had boarded her were taken off, and she was taken in tow. The tow parted in the early hours of the following day, but despite the initial report she did not immediately sink, but stayed afloat until the next day. [4]

In December 1982, a report on the loss of the *Atlantic Conveyor* was produced by the Ministry of Defence for Cunard Line's use. An opinion on that report was provided by Captain H J Holdrup, who was Cunard's marine superintendent at the time. He commented that Cunard had no alternative but to accept the findings of the inquiry, which he described as 'painstaking and comprehensive', commenting that 'it is doubtful if the subject could have been as well covered by any other investigative body.' He went on to say that there are

---

[4] See the more detailed account of the *Irishman*'s towing of the *Atlantic Conveyor* in Chapter 6.

'virtually no criticisms of either the ship or her Cunard crew in this report. The contrary exists in as much as great play is made of the high degree of cooperation which existed between the Royal Naval and merchant naval personnel.' He concluded: 'the conclusion of satisfaction must be arrived at, following close study of this report. *Atlantic Conveyor* did all that was expected of her; her crew did more. No further comment is necessary.'

On 16 June 2007 a memorial to those who lost their lives on the *Atlantic Conveyor* was unveiled at Cape Pembroke in the Falkland Islands. The unveiling, by HRH Prince Edward, was also attended by Charles Drought. The memorial, formed by a propeller from HMS *Protector*, is situated so that, looking between the two upraised propeller blades, a bearing of 062° magnetic points in the direction where the *Atlantic Conveyor* is lying, 90 miles out.

Atlantic Causeway

A sister ship to the *Atlantic Conveyor*, she was one of a class of six built to the same basic design. They were the only two of the six under the British flag; the others were divided between the Swedish, French and Dutch flags,[5] as part of the Atlantic Container Line consortium. As she was converted after her sister ship, some of the conversion works reflected the lessons learnt on the *Conveyor*, but her purpose was the same: to carry helicopters and stores, which her particular design equipped her for.

The accounts of the losses of *Sir Galahad*, HMS *Sheffield*, HMS *Coventry*, and to a lesser extent the *Atlantic Conveyor*, are known and recorded. The account of the *Atlantic Causeway* is one that is, fortunately for her crew at the time, less exciting – although for those whose first experience of war it was, still exciting enough. Like the majority of the merchant ships taken up from trade, her crew were not injured, the ship was not attacked; she did her job and returned. However, through the eyes of her master and her young radio officer, the excitement of that

---

[5] E C Talbot-Booth, *Talbot-Booth's Merchant Ships*. London, 1979, Vol.1, 118.

period is brought vividly to life.

The master's tale

Captain Michael Twomey was the master throughout the period of her deployment. He had spent his entire seagoing career with Port Line and its subsequent changes of name and ownership within the Cunard Group. He was the archetypical ship's master, bearded, charming and with a wonderful sense of humour. He was interviewed by the author in 2008,[6] and described his experiences of that time.

> She was converted in a most remarkable six days in Devonport dockyard from being a transatlantic roll-on/roll-off container ship into what I like to think was a fairly efficient helicopter carrier, no fixed-wing aircraft unfortunately, although I did try to lure one on one day but he wouldn't come. We had a naval party of over 100; we had a few Portakabins stuck on for extra accommodation and the rest just doubled up. We had eight helicopter pilots in the second mate's cabin. They were big cabins! The rest just jammed in wherever we could put them because the normal ship's company was something like 30.
>
> There was an enormous amount of very creditable work done by our shore staff, who gelled very well with the naval stores department. Our catering department did a magnificent job, in fact. The decks were flattened and anything that stuck up like ventilators and fan motors and things like that were all cut off so we had virtually a flat deck. We had to cut the container lashing boxes and helicopter fixing points were put in their place. We had two flight decks, one on the forward deck, of course, which was our major one, and another one aft of the accommodation; there were difficulties with that because

---

[6] D Smith and J Johnson-Allen, *Voices from the Bridge*. Rendlesham, 2010, 171.

of the funnel fumes and the turbulence caused by the superstructure and the fact that there was a ramp sticking up above the level of the deck by about six feet, so when we were operating helicopters we had to lower the stern ramp level with the deck. There again, we used the ramp to run landing craft up on when we were there but it wasn't considered strong enough so we had to move anchor cable so that the anchor cable supported the ramp, which were all fairly major undertakings and all done in six days.

We filled up with fuel and 3000 tons of everything the army needed. The only hiccup was our aircraft refuelling system. We used whisky containers, the tanks that were shipped across to the United States so ACL, the container company that operated that service, gave us all their spare whisky tanks, which we then had to connect up with flexible couplings because the containers moved very slightly, which caused a bit of a problem to us because we couldn't get the flexible couplings tight. The ship was awash with avgas. At the end of the operation, when we had thrown a wingding on our return to Devonport for the dockyard staff, who had done a magnificent job, I said as much to them. The yard manager said to me that everybody was involved in finding the flexible couplings that leaked and needed the O rings which we had asked for. We had wanted lots and lots and lots of them. He said that every plumber from Bristol to Land's End had a policeman beating on his door in the middle of the night saying get down to your shop because we need all your O rings. We had just sent a signal saying we need O rings and they kept appearing – we didn't know where they had come from because we were all a bit busy. It just shows the involvement of everybody in that conflict. It touched everyone. Normally, to get anything out of the naval stores department takes weeks and sheaves of paper. One telephone call, be on a truck within an hour sir, and with you in six. That was the sort of level at which it was worked. The paper went out of the window.

Did the helicopters land on you?

Yes, we went out into Mount's Bay and anchored there and they all arrived. The rotors folded when they were on deck. The *Atlantic Causeway* was 700 feet long and 26,000 tons, which was bigger than a Royal Naval aircraft carrier. We were the biggest things there.

When the helicopters landed on, were you aware of their arrival?

No, not really. It was a lovely, lovely day. That was a test run. We were doing 12 knots. That photograph is of me, with the bald patch, on the bridge wing, with the senior naval officer. I was a captain RNR, which was a great help to me although I was serving as a Merchant Navy captain. I did know a few of the naval officers who were there.

Although we did not normally land Chinooks on board, we did occasionally, on the after deck, which does show the size of the after deck. We were anchored in San Carlos Water. Although there were air attacks and it got very noisy we were not ourselves attacked. I acquired some ex-Argentinian rapid-firing rifles quite illicitly by swapping them with the commodore for a helicopter. The Royal Navy had supplied us with blast protection gear in case we were attacked. We had an aircraft repair team on board so damaged aircraft came to us for repair. As far as the weather went it was blessed, it was a normal South Atlantic weather, but, on the day of surrender winter appeared and it snowed. We brought four Argentinian Pucara aircraft back with us, which were scattered round the country, one to the naval museum at Yeovilton ...

So we came back to the UK and I came home on well-earned leave. She was restored to normal operating condition. 825 Squadron, the Sea King squadron, sent the senior pilot thereof up on the way home. 'We would like you to have a little memento of our stay on board, sir'. I said, 'That's very kind of you, old boy.' There was a chap with him, sort of staggering with something and he said we thought you might stick it on the wall of the officers' lounge ... It was an Argentinian rocket launcher with a rocket in it. I had just received a signal to say that we were going to Belfast so I had to say that is extremely kind of you, very thoughtful, but I don't think we ought to take it to Belfast because it might have been a bit unpopular, so it was unceremoniously ditched over the side.

Michael Twomey had another, rather special, memory of this time:

Whilst the *Atlantic Causeway* was anchored in San Carlos Water, the *Sir Galahad* was struck by an Argentinian Exocet missile. There were many casualties, and what were described as the 'walking wounded' were sent to her for treatment. 'All the men were from the Welsh Guards and all marched on board. Looking at them, I felt that it was only because they were the Guards that they were able to walk at all. They were taken to the officers' bar and laid down to make sure that everything was in order. As I walked in, in my uniform with badges of rank on my shoulders, they all tried to stand up.

The radio officer's tale

Among the papers that Captain Michael Twomey had kept from his period in the ship, a copy of the journal kept by Steve Cockburn, who was the ship's radio officer, was discovered. This commenced on the day that *Atlantic Causeway* was taken up from trade, on 4 May, and ended on the day before she returned to Devonport on 25 July. Also included are copies of the naval party's daily orders and the international news received on board by the radio officer, for the crew's information.

The journal reflects one man's views of events as they

occurred. The radio officer occupied a rather lonely place on board. Answerable only to the master, on many ships he was employed not by the company on whose ship he sailed but by a separate company, for example Marconi, who supplied both the equipment and the operator. Keeping his own watch pattern, he was in a good position to observe events and to have access to all the information coming into his headphones. As such he was also in a position of great trust, as in many cases only he and the master were privy to the signals coming aboard. Steve Cockburn had joined the ship at short notice, having just married and returned from honeymoon; his previous ship had been a cruise liner based in the Caribbean. His journal starts on a low key on 4 May:

> Today the news was heard on the BBC that the ship was to be requisitioned. The vessel arrived at the pilot off Southampton and took him aboard. It was then that we were told to turn around and go to Antwerp to discharge all of our cargo. Also from there we were to proceed to Devonport Naval Dockyard, Plymouth for structural alterations to prepare us for our new task. We dropped off the pilot again and carried on to Antwerp, where we arrived at night.

After discharging in Antwerp, they arrived in Devonport on 6 May and the conversion started:

> At approximately 18.00 hours we moved into the dry dock and it was then swarms of workers arrived to start the work agenda.

Two days later, on Saturday 8 May:

> Work has been frantically continuing as ship is altered to suit the needs of the helicopters which we will apparently be carrying. The dry dock level has been highered [sic] and stores are being loaded in a virtually endless supply. On the lower decks are all the digging and general Royal Engineers stores. Satellite communications area has been sited above the bridge and communications equipment is being installed in the new radio room (ex-pilots cabin). The

workmen are working at an even faster pace, and it is obvious that we are to put to sea as soon as it is humanly possible.

Sunday was not a day of rest:

Work furiously continues and it seems quite incredible that so many men know what they are doing. You very rarely seen one of them standing still, yet there are hundreds of men welding, sawing, pull[ing] down bulkheads and deckheads, running cables, moving gear and all the time a continuing clear-up operation, removing all used discarded or useless materials and packing.

From the next entry in his journal it appeared that he was involved in the recording of the sweets and general stores that were taken on board for use. A list in the journal shows that, among other items, 1440 Mars Bars, 576 rolls of Polo Mints, 864 chocolate bars, 108 toothbrushes, 48 pairs of underpants, 384 packets of aspirin, 200 packets of razor blades and 96 bottles of aftershave were carried. In addition it also loaded alcohol, including 350 bottles of gin, 590 bottles of whiskey, 225 bottles of brandy and over 55,000 cans of beer and, last but not least, 210,000 cigarettes. This was for a crew of approximately 140. As an interesting comparison, the 170 crew of the frigate HMS *Ambuscade* consumed during her deployment at the Falklands, over 83 days, 25,812 bars of chocolate and 345,000 cigarettes, but only 19,200 cans of beer.[7] The *QE2* had sailed with 3 million Mars Bars.

The conversion continued, and by 13 May the works had been substantially completed:

In the early hours of the morning the decks were cleared and the ship prepared to move out of the dry dock. We eventually left dry dock around 08.00 and moved out into the Sound, off Plymouth, with the aid of tugs. The hangar had been basically completed with the roof fitted into position and huge sliding doors on. The huge expanse of

---

[7] J Lippiett, *War and Peas*. Bosham, 2007, 277.

deck was painted green with a helicopter landing circle in the middle and similarly the aft deck was completed. At midday a heavy lift crane came alongside on the port side. We commenced to load more stores directly onto the main fore deck. This, however, had the disadvantage that we had to wait until the crane moved (which was eventually about 14.00) before we could receive helicopters ...

At about 14.20 the first helicopter arrived and was stowed in the forward hangar. The eventual number was 28 (20 Wessex and 8 Sea King) and they proceed[ed] to land at an incredible rate. The Wessex arrived first but they only have four pilots therefore every fourth one needs to return to base with the pilots. They were all on board installed by 21.00 hours with two being placed on the aft flight deck and the rest on the foredeck and in the hangar. The speed at which a helicopter landed and was stowed, complete with all its protective clothing, was quite unbelievable, particularly as the crew have not worked together before. To us the helicopters landing and the way in which it was facilitated was fascinating. I do not think any of us could really comprehend what was happening but it was undoubtedly an event none would forget. We sailed the next morning with a very full ship. Extra cabins had been built directly off the main accommodation where there used to be deck and portable cabins have been sited on the aft end of the superstructure.

They left the anchorage the next day, and the first day at sea was a happy one:

Ship left the anchorage in the early hours of the morning. It was not until breakfast that the amount of crew on board was really appreciated. The dining room was full of men all trying to be served food and find somewhere to sit after they had received. It was all good-spirited and though everyone was, naturally, a bit wary of each other everything was good-hearted. Throughout the day men were moving everywhere over the ship finding out where everything was and ensuring everything had been secured correctly. At lunchtime there was [sic] again some small problems but everything was becoming a lot smoother and a schedule is now being run so that certain groups of men went to eat at certain times. The weather is excellent and everyone is in high spirits although everyone is apprehensive about how far we are actually going to go. We think we are offloading at Ascension Island but no one knows anything for definite.

At approximately 19.00 we had a ship come alongside us while we were still making headway. She was the RFA ship *Grey Rover* and there was an exercise performed by passing a fuel line across by crane and ropes onto our ship. This was to see whether we could actually be fuelled at sea and it is termed a RAS (replenishment at sea).

After everything had been secured ships officers were invited by the aircraft pilots for drinks in the wardroom and some new friendships were struck as everyone become better acquainted. It was a very good evening and all enjoyed themselves. There was much talk about helicopters, the ship, where we were going, the war, and, of course, lots of joviality and singing, especially as the evening progressed.

They had embarked a naval party, which totalled 109. As already mentioned, two Portakabins had been provided, as on the *Atlantic Conveyor*, but in addition two annexes to the superstructure were added. In total, these additional areas accommodated over 60 of the naval party. A further 29 were accommodated in existing cabins and the balance bunked in the sports room. The helicopters on board were from two different squadrons: 825, which flew Sea Kings and had thirteen officers, and 847, which flew Wessex helicopters and had four officers.

The voyage continued, and the enlarged crew settled in to a routine. However, he notes:

The new Royal Navy ideas are strange to us all and the

amount of information given on notice boards is amazing. To ensure knowledge of what is happening constant monitoring of this information is necessary.

The days were enlivened by various activities – lifeboat and emergency drills, of course, but also more unusual activities for the Merchant Navy members of the crew:

Another beautiful day – weatherwise. In the morning there was pistol shooting at targets on the aft deck. This was a weapon training session held by a commando colour sergeant. Anyone was welcome to have a go and quite a few of us did just that. In the afternoon we had a real sight as the helicopter pilots and crews had training sessions. These exercises consist of flying helicopters (one Wessex and one Sea King) off both the flight decks in all directions and then landing them back, again, at different angles and by varying methods. With such good weather it was another sight that was not to be missed. The flights started about 13.30 and throughout the afternoon the ship kept changing course in different wind directions to enable the pilots to exercise under varying conditions. They were taking off and landing about every 5 minutes and as the afternoon passed the ground crews became noticeably more efficient.

Helicopter exercises continued. For the first time, night landing and taking off were practised:

[They] recommenced with night flying exercises between 19.30 and 20.30. Here again we were treated to a wonderful sight as the Wessex and Sea King landed and took off with the minimum amount of lights being used. Some spotlights are directed downwards to light the landing spots but the rest of the ship is in total darkness with a full blackout being enforced. Lights have been rigged on the mastheads to enable the pilots to see where they are. To see a flashing light appear and then a helicopter loom out of the darkness and land is a really unnerving experience and the reality of the whole situation is beginning to dawn on us all.

Like the *Atlantic Conveyor*, they called at Freetown to take bunkers. They arrived at 20.00 and sailed at 08.00 the next day. There was no shore leave allowed so although Steve Cockburn commented that the scenery was beautiful, no closer inspection was possible. On the day they sailed from Freetown the ship's crew were offered the chance for a flight in a helicopter:

> The first five or six crew members went up without any mishaps but [were] helped to enjoy it by a bit of stunt work in the form of very sharp turning. When they had offloaded, the helicopter was called to land and suddenly the fire bells started. There was rather pandemonium as men went to the wrong place. The exercise actually turned out to be a real fire but it was successfully put out by one of the engineers. Drills will be in store for us now I think ... The whole day was yet another reminder that we were now a warship.

The next Saturday, 22 May, was an eventful day:

> Early this morning we sighted the *QE2* just ahead of us. We have on board 20 Wessex helicopters and only four pilots for them so we presumed that there would be even more men arriving to join us. Instead of going into Ascension, as was expected, we carried on steaming and stores were taken from us to the *QE2*, as well as stores being sent out from Ascension. Due to the news of the landing on the Falklands of our troops, the *QE2* was steaming at full speed down there and we were given the same directive. At least now we know how far south we are going and it certainly looks like the whole way.
>
> The *QE2* could really do with our aircraft to offload the 3000 troops she is carrying. The radar spares that were needed for the RN modified radar did not arrive from UK as expected and consequently a helicopter had to fly to the *QE2*, which was now at full speed and leaving us behind, to pick up the necessary parts. A good point today,

and certainly a cheerful boost to all, was the arrival of our first mail. Though it is not long since we left Devonport, so much has happened that it feels like a very long time apart from our respective families and loved ones. The benefit to us all now is, of course, the fact that we are on 150 per cent bonus each so that is naturally a boost. The war bonus applied since we went over 7 degrees south and remains in force until the conflict is over or we return north of this point.

Despite the lack of defensive equipment on the *Atlantic Conveyor*, which caused Charles Drought such great concern (see 'The engineer's tale'), the *Atlantic Causeway* was better provided for, with two machine guns mounted on each bridge wing and a further two in reserve. Two days later the reality of the situation became more apparent:

This afternoon we were called to action stations and all types of drills were carried out as we all found out exactly where we had to go and what to do there. The machine guns on the bridge wings were used in mock-up air attacks and fires were fought all over the ship. Medical and stretcher parties were also in full use. This really is no joke. I do not think any of us thought we will come down this far or that we were to become acting parts of a warship. We are now under military laws and can consider ourselves as full members of Her Majesty's fighting forces. I do not really believe anyone thought this was going to happen. Still, we are here now and we have got to pull together and ensure that we know as much as we need to carry out our jobs efficiently as possible – for everyone's sake.

On 26 May they learnt of the loss of the *Atlantic Conveyor*, which had occurred the previous day:

And then, on the 12.00 BBC News, the tragic news of the loss of HMS *Coventry* and our sister *Atlantic Conveyor* was disclosed. The shock was quite amazing. I think mainly to us because it was the first merchant vessel to be hit and also because she was so close to us with many good friends on her. The fact she took two Exocet missiles and still managed to abandon ship is good news but four are dead and we hope it is not friends. Everyone is now dressed in action gear and we all carry our survival kit with us at all times. The sense of danger is even closer now.

By the Saturday, they had arrived about 250 miles from the Falklands, where they met HMS *Bristol*, which was to be their escort. The weather had worsened, but nevertheless orders came for some of the helicopters to leave:

In the mid-morning news arrived that four of the Sea King helicopters with pilots and ground crew were to fly. They were to stop on HMS *Hermes* for fuel and then carry on to the Falkland Islands. Hurriedly the aircraft were made ready to fly, loaded with necessary stores and equipment.

During the night the weather had become quite rough and we were now in about force 6 or 7. The swell was rolling the ship a lot and the wind was becoming stronger. Also we had lost a boiler and consequently our top speed was only about 16 knots. To remain in the zone and also remain under the watchful eye of HMS *Bristol* we had to alter course as directed by her. This caused a lot more rolling by the ship and this was further added to when we had to change course continually to have the wind in the correct direction for the helicopters to take off. By 13.00 the bridge was full of people doing all sorts of communications work and directing activities. A Wessex (aft) was prepared as well and this was used as a search and rescue craft. At 14.35 the first Sea King took off as well as the Wessex. The Sea King tried to make a landing on the after deck but was waved up again as it became precariously close to the tail ramp due to the turbulence of the now very strong wind, whipping around the superstructure. Eventually all four Sea Kings and crew had left and our best luck goes with them all. It will certainly seem quiet without them all.

On the next day they received orders to head directly for the

Falklands:

> We were given orders at about 11.45 to head directly to the Falklands and, in convoy with the *Europic Ferry* and HMS *Bristol*, did so. Everyone started making ready for offloading and also mentally preparing themselves for what was ahead. The pressure is certainly beginning to show with one or two of the men on board … It is obvious that we are being treated more carefully now since the loss of the *Conveyor*. At 17.00 all hell let loose as we were called to action stations with an air raid warning – RED, meaning that we were directly a target. We did not have an escort now because *Bristol* had carried on with the *Europic Ferry*. Everyone waited anxiously, but by 18.00 the warning was graded at YELLOW and we were stood down.

On the last day of the month, the tension increased to a new level:

> Today, we started off in the holding zone again with lots of other ships. The sea is rough and the ship is being thrown about quite a lot with severe rolling as we continually change course. At first light we sent a Sea King across to the *Nordic Ferry* to transfer more men to our ship. By 11.35 the first load had arrived and more followed. Suddenly we were given a course which was to start us on our way into the Falklands. During the afternoon we passed through the main bulk of the Task Force where all the main ships were, including HMS *Hermes* and *Canberra*. Our guarding ship now was HMS *Brilliant* and we were in convoy with three other vessels. We continued our course without any mishap and arrived at our destination early in the morning. The tension on the ship is high now. There are a lot of men on here and still we do not know exactly what we are doing. We know we are to offload but how long we are going to stop in is not yet known.

The month of June started with the *Atlantic Causeway* at anchor in San Carlos Water:

It was pitch black until about 10.30 so the only time we were able to see anything was when the black silhouettes of the surrounding ships and the slopes of the land started to creep into view ... The men had started preparing to offload and by first light the helicopters started flying off laden with troops and stores. The Mexeflotes pulled up behind us and the required cargo was driven off onto them and taken ashore. This continued all day with helicopters being prepared, loaded and flown off and the decks being emptied. We were due to leave tonight but it eventually was disclosed that we were to continue to unload throughout the night and further instructions about our leaving time was to be passed on to us. At about 13.00 we were called to action stations which was an air raid warning red, and in this particular spot that meant a lot.

We now all work as an efficient team and were soon prepared as best we could be. One of the Argentinian planes had been shot down by rifles so a lot of them had appeared on the bridge. I think everyone wanted to be the one to hit a plane. We were eventually stood down and apparently seven Argentinian planes were reported to have been shot down by our forces ... It has been a busy day with many tired faces around. Our upper decks are bare expanses now – good luck all! We have not come under fire yet – I wonder what tomorrow will bring?

The newsletter for the day, as well as current local news also noted that the Pope on his visit to Britain celebrated an open-air mass in Glasgow. More relevantly, it had started:

Troops have advanced to within 12 miles of Port Stanley. MoD said that fighting was going on in the Mount Kent area which slopes down to Port Stanley. 3000 more troops are said to have landed on the north side – presumably the regiments off the *QE2*. Harriers attacked Stanley airfield again yesterday and a number of light aircraft are believed to have been damaged. Details about Sunday's bombing say that two Exocets were believed to have been fired and shot down by our fire. No ships were hit. The *Atlantic Conveyor* (our sister) has now sunk I am afraid chaps. It is still not known whether any of the supplies on board were salvaged.

2 June continued as the previous day, with Steve Cockburn noting:

Offloading has continued throughout the night and we now appear to be rid of all the Rapier missiles we have been carrying and that is a bit of a relief as they could have proved very dangerous had we been hit. The most welcome sight today, however, had to be the very low mist cover which was making flying very hazardous and duly made it a very good fog screen for our ships. We have moved position during the night but just as it was becoming lighter, about 10.00, we moved back down to our original [position]. As we weighed anchor, however, the white structure of a ship could be seen directly ahead of us and this proved to be the *Canberra* which had arrived in overnight to discharge her cargo of men which was the Fifth Regiment [*sic*] consisting of the Scots and Welsh Guards and the mighty Gurkhas. There are about 3000 of them so our forces are certainly being strengthened now.

Throughout the day we continued discharging cargo and large areas of space started to appear below decks. Also, as we had so much aviation fuel on board we became a sort of petrol station for all sorts of helicopters – Sea Kings, Wessex, Scouts, Wasps, as well as the helicopters which called in with men for a beer, or shower, or to buy items from the purser. The constant flow of men, all in high spirits, proved to be a great boost to us all as we were passed information about the fighting and recounted various tales of events ...

At 22.00 we weighed anchor along with a number of other ships. HMS *Plymouth* led us out, followed by *Sir Bedivere* (RFA), MV *Norland*, *Baltic Ferry*, then we followed on with *Sir Galahad* (RFA) bringing up the rear ... It is not often that you see ships playing follow the leader like this – especially with the leader giving all the instructions.

The next few days were spent in the holding zone, 250 miles from the Falklands Islands, so they were able to relax:

> Whatever was happening on the Falklands, and we knew our troops were ready to take Port Stanley, there did not seem to be too much to worry about being 250 miles away from it all.

However, on the 4th, refuelling was required for the ship, so RFA *Olmeda* came alongside:

> and the necessary lines were fired over. By about 13.00 we had the pipeline strung between us and the pumping of fuel commenced, or so it should have been, but almost immediately they called for us to use the emergency release (an 'emergency breakaway'). There was some trouble in doing this and before it was actually done they told us everything was all right. The reason was that they had had a fire in their pump room but fortunately it was brought under control quickly. Pumping commenced. The pipeline is supported by a strong wire jackstay from the derrick on their ship across to the RAS mast on ours. About half an hour after pumping started the jackstay broke, which seemed quite dangerous but the pipe was still quite well supported and still suspended out of the water so pumping continued ... We finished pumping at about 16.30 and soon after all was disconnected ... We did manage to swap some of our films with her, however, so we all look forward to some different picture shows. The weather is reasonably calm and I do not really think anyone is too bothered to be out of the way of the main action. In this situation, however, thoughts can tend towards home and speculation starts about how long we will be here.

They joined the main Task Force on 7 June and took on board three Sea King helicopters which were used as part of the anti-submarine screen for the Carrier Battle Group.

Basically we were acting like a floating garage and throughout the day helicopters kept arriving, filling up with fuel and flying off again.

On 8 June they returned to San Carlos and their first experience of war:

At 11.00 we were called to action stations with a red alert due to unidentified electronic emissions not far away. [Added in a different hand, 'suspected ground-based Exocet from Pebble Island. Evasive action taken.'] ... More was to come.

Although the afternoon was relatively quiet for the *Causeway*, in the early evening action stations were called more than once. During the day RFA *Sir Galahad* had been struck by Exocet missiles and the ship was abandoned. The following excerpt describes very vividly the care given to the survivors:

19.25 saw us return to a precautionary action state as reports of unidentified emissions came in again. We all stood waiting for more reports when we were asked if we could take ten walking wounded. We said yes and soon after they arrived by helicopter. Shortly afterwards we were asked to take more and approximately another ten arrived. This was a time when the full realities of the horrors of war came home to everyone and was also a time when the merchantmen on board showed their total adaptability. The casualties that arrived were off *Sir Galahad* which had been hit a few times already and today was very badly hit. The men on board were the Welsh Guards and at the time they were preparing to disembark to go ashore. The men that came on here had suffered quite severe burning to the hands and face; it appears that they were not issued with anti-flash gear so these burns must be attributed to this. They had all 'blacked-up', ready to go ashore and with burnt clothing, burnt hands and faces, singed hair and melted over jackets they were quite horrific to see.

At first we were all at a bit of a loss as to what to do

and the doctor and medic had their task cut out administering drugs and injections. Everything that they needed was immediately carried or fetched but really we were unable to help much. Then the doctor asked for buckets of cold disinfected water and explained how we were to cool the burns and cut off all excess skin. Immediately, many willing hands set to work changing blistered, charred skin to clean, albeit painful, exposed skin. All their faces were washed down, as well, and generally they were made as comfortable as possible. Some had burns on the back of the legs and buttocks and no modesty was allowed as the burnt clothing was cut away and the blisters cooled and dressed. Admittedly, no one was complaining so it could not have been too bad.

As each man was cleaned up to a reasonable state we took him to a cabin where we could take his old clothes off and give him a good wash before re-dressing him in the 'survivors', clothes that we had on board, issued by the Navy. After this he was sat in the purser's cabin where hot tea and a welcome chat with his friends about all that had occurred.

This process carried on until very late in the morning, as the more severe cases took longer to do. However everyone stuck to it and gradually all the men were seen to and bunked down with clean gear on. The doctor had a look at each one individually and although two had to be put on drips the rest were comfortable as possible either in the sports room (which had been emptied of pilots) or in the officer's bar on stretchers. The most that we could do was done and we all drifted off slowly and left the rest to the professionals – doctor and medic – but the horrible realities remained in our mind and one always wonders what tomorrow will bring but, as for today, full credit must be given to the men on board for working hard, long hours and succeeding excellently in a task which they have never really been trained for. And tomorrow – well, we will wait and see. We are in the middle of it all now so the sooner it is all over the better. If everyone carries on like this though, we have really got a good chance.

The next day, 9 June, the offloading continued while the wounded were being cared for:

The wounded were in a much better state this morning and were constantly tended, wiped, cleaned and fed by the doctor and other willing helpers. They were made as comfortable as possible, whilst we tried to find out when they would be transported to the *Uganda* – hospital ship. At 18.05 the alarm bells sounded for 'action red' which did not come to anything but did, however, manage to put everyone really back on edge as if we were not already. Suddenly a Sea King arrived and wanted the wounded so although we had had no prior warning whatsoever we took as many as we could out to him immediately then brought the rest, along with their gear, later. They were all able to walk to the helicopter which seemed quite amazing as some had become quite swollen and sore as the burns had puffed them up and wept continually.

As soon as all the casualties were offloaded, the first of the survivors from RFA ships *Sir Galahad* and *Sir Tristram* began to arrive.. We had been informed that we would receive just over 100 and had made plans as best we could but we were really overrun with about 170 men arrived. There were many Chinese crew members amongst them as well. They arrived by landing craft at the stern ramp and we had quite a job trying to organise them. Primarily we filled the officers' bar area with Chinese and then filled the crew's bar whilst the overspill were told to sit in the corridors and on stairs while we tried to sort them out. We managed to find captains and pursers from the respective ships which helped ... At 22.00 we sailed from San Carlos with quite a ship full and everyone settled to as good a night's sleep as they could possibly get.

Tomorrow we are supposed to offload all of them to

another ship, presumably *Canberra*, which we believe will take them to Ascension ... Anyway we shall have to see what tomorrow will bring but for tonight they are at least warm, dry and being fed but we will not be able to maintain this amount of people for a very long period of time.'

The transfer of the survivors commenced two days later:

The transfer is scheduled for 16.00 and is to be to two tankers, the *British Test* and the *British Trent*.

However, things did not go quite according to plan:

Eventually ... we managed to get a Sea King to start the transfer. It turned out that only 75 were to be moved to the *British Test* and this was mainly the men from *Sir Galahad*. At approximately 17.00 the actual transfer started and groups of the survivors were kitted out in once only suits and led them to the helicopter which took them over ... the men were transferred very quickly once everything got going properly.

While all this was going on, they were in the middle of the Task Force with activity all around them:

A typical sight today was: a Wessex or Sea King landing or taking off on the fore and aft deck, HMS *Broadsword* very close to us as escort. The *Hermes* and *Invincible* off to one side. Other Royal or merchant vessels around and, at one point as the sun began to set, a merchant and RFA vessel doing a RAS sailed very close across our bows ... It was announced that night was going to be the start of our major offensive against Port Stanley ... Tomorrow should be another interesting day, as if every other one wasn't!

The following day the remaining survivors were transferred to the *British Trent*, which was to take them to Ascension Island.

The BBC news received the next day, 13 June, reported that:

Britain says that its forces have advanced five miles towards Port Stanley and the Argentinians have said that their forces had been forced to retreat. The Argentinians have said that they had suffered high losses and they say that the British forces have also suffered high casualties. MoD say, however, the British losses appear to have been light. Hard fighting is reported, however, and reports in London say that more than 300 Argentinian prisoners have been taken.

The next day the crew of *Atlantic Causeway* took part in a re-storing exercise, but the day ended on a high note. The start was a RAS with RFA *Tidepool*, which started about 12.30:

Whilst pumping was going on we had *Tidepool* on our starboard side, *Tor Caledonia* (a merchant vessel belonging to Tor Lloyd) on our starboard quarter and directly behind us was RFA vessel *Stromness*. Thus, whilst we were pumping, the Wessex was able to re-store us from the two other vessels at the same time. As the afternoon wore on the wind became stronger and was bitterly cold. The seas became rougher and by the time we had disconnected and moved away from the *Tidepool* there was heavy rain, high winds and the sea was becoming quite bad [in a different hand is noted 'emergency breakaway due heavy weather'] … The highlight … was announced by the SNO when he told us all that 'the white flag was flying over Port Stanley', which were the words we had all [been] waiting for.

The gale continued for the next two days. During that period a telegram was received from the Admiralty advising that 'The Falkland islands are repossessed' and congratulating all who had played a part in the operation. Further orders were also received, instructing them to proceed towards Port Stanley, where:

… as had been expressed on the news, there was a lot of hardship due to the amount of men captured (14,000 Argentinian prisoners) with the shortage of supplies, food, shelter and bad weather conditions. We were to sail to Port William, off Stanley Harbour, and our instructions were 'to be ready on arrival to provide shelter from the elements and sustenance for large numbers of our own troops or Prisoners of War'.

The following day they arrived in Port Stanley and anchored in their designated position:

The lights around Port Stanley could be clearly seen. The ship was still rolling quite heavily as the heavy swell continued. At dawn, which was around 10.30, we were able to start making out the land around us and by the time light was with us the line of ships right the way up into the harbour could plainly be seen.

Despite their orders no troops, either British or Argentinian, arrived until they were advised that 'we would only be taking our own troops for rest and recreation after their hardships'. Presumably by that time they had realised that orders were likely to change with little warning, so they nevertheless prepared the ship in case prisoners of war were sent to them. They prepared a large area on 'B' deck, which was roped off. Pipes were run down to the deck to pump hot air, and tables were set up to serve food. 'Buckets have been provided for latrines and, though primitive, at least anyone staying there will be warm, dry and fed.'

Despite their preparations, the following days passed in a similar pattern, with *Atlantic Causeway* acting as a refuelling point for helicopters, and providing a break for their crews, so they could have showers and meals. Many other ships were also anchored nearby. Steve Cockburn noted that on the 22nd, on their port beam were two ships (*Canberra* and *Contender Bezant*), a further two (*St Edmund* and *Elk*) were in Port Stanley Harbour, and on their starboard side were a further seven (HMS *Fearless*, HMS *Penelope*, RFA *Stromness* and MVs *Uganda*, *Fort Toronto*, *Norland* and *Licon* [*Lycaon*]).

On the Friday of that week,, which had otherwise been relatively uneventful, they refilled with fresh water from the *Fort Toronto*, the tanker which had been taken up for the sole purpose of providing fresh water to the Task Force. Being in port meant that the *Atlantic Causeway*, which like all ships normally made her own fresh water, was unable to do so. After that she was refuelled with avcat (aviation fuel) from the RFA

Blue Rover. The month ended with rough weather, preventing the discharge of cargo either by landing craft or by helicopter. The crew enjoyed a day's 'make and mend' (doing necessary domestic chores).

July opened with an easing of better weather and a small drama, when 'man overboard' was called. In the waters of the South Atlantic life expectancy is short for a human, so the presence of a helicopter meant that the time from falling in to landing back on the deck was less than two minutes, and the man was none the worse for his immersion.

The days continued to pass without much incident. On 10 July they commenced loading helicopters for the return trip. These were not the only aircraft to be shipped:

Early in the afternoon the first Pucara arrived. This was an Argentinian plane and we were shipping two of them to the UK for museum pieces. The first was lowered on board by Chinook.

By 13 July they had moved to San Carlos Water and were completing the loading of helicopters, including two Argentinian Iroquois, and three Argentinian Mercedes trucks. At 17.00 they sailed for the United Kingdom.

The return trip was relaxing; sports took place on deck as the weather improved. They arrived at Ascension Island on 20 July, receiving mail, which was a pleasure, and disembarking some of the naval party, who would fly the rest of the way home. The naval daily orders advertised a race meeting to be held on the following Saturday. On the following day they crossed the equator, at 25 knots. The naval party amused themselves by engaging in clay pigeon shooting, to expend loose ammunition.

On Saturday 24 July:

Today was an excellent day, enjoyment wise, when the horseracing meet took place on the after deck ... At 14.00 the horseracing commenced and this turned out to be very good fun. There had obviously been some hard work put in and the track had been marked out, horses and jumps had been made ... Much betting and frivolity took place and the MC was the buffer [chief bosun's mate, of the naval party], of course. After the racing there was an absolutely excellent barbecue, run by the cooks and that is very much appreciated.

Prizes were to be awarded for 'best hat', 'most outrageous costume' and 'prettiest lady?'

The journal finishes on the day before they arrived in Devonport, and concludes:

At night there was some small celebration of goodbye but nothing too raucous as we have an early start tomorrow and it will be a very long day.

The activities for the next day are recorded in the daily orders for that day. They were to have anchored in Mount's Bay at 04.00, weighing anchor three hours later and arriving alongside about 12.00, where they were met by the Flag Officer Plymouth and the families, who came on board.

For the next 20 years Steve Cockburn, in between spells of varied shore-going employment, which included obtaining a degree and qualifying as a chartered surveyor, continued to work at sea in various companies as a radio officer, finally coming ashore in 1999.

4

The tankers

British Trent

British Tay

Eburna

British Trent

The 'River' class, including the *British Trent* and the *British Tay*, were 25,000 ton product-carrying ships. They were designed with pipeline layouts to allow for the carriage of several different grades of petroleum products without contamination. This was a common design to all tankers that carried refined products, rather than the single cargo of crude oil carried by very large crude carriers (VLCC). The design of this class had been earmarked for the potential refuelling of warships at sea, after tests were carried out in the 1970s to assess their suitability.

Various River class ships participated in NATO exercises and practised replenishment at sea (RAS) in the Western approaches to the English Channel. How much of this training was actually undertaken is questioned in an account from a Royal Fleet Auxiliary officer who was seconded to another of the class:

> Looking back it seems strange that although the Ministry of whatever was involved in the designs of the ships, it seems nobody thought to give some basic, regular training to the officers and crew. Most of them had no idea of how the Navy was controlled, or how a Task Force operated.[1]

With the benefit of first-hand experience of the company in question, the author can well imagine that the commercial pressures of operating tankers gave little, if any, time for training about the Royal Navy, or indeed any knowledge of the operation of a task force!

Two of the class, the *British Esk* and the *British Tamar*, were modified by the installation of appropriate equipment for stern refuelling and were therefore able to refuel by this method; the others were able to undertake replenishment at sea (RAS) beam-to-beam. By 1982, twelve River class ships were still owned by BP. Of these, four were either in inaccessible locations or unavailable for use due to existing charters. The

---

[1] G Puddefoot, *No Sea too Rough*. London, 2007, 13.

MoD therefore indicated that rather than requisition the ships it would charter the eight available.

The *British Trent* was in the Mediterranean so, on completion of the discharge of her cargo at Livorno, in Italy, she sailed for the United Kingdom on 7 April and arrived at Portsmouth on the 12th. At that time, in common with all the other BP ships that were chartered, the cadets, junior ratings and wives were removed, and a full crew change was undertaken. This ensured that all who were to sail were volunteers.

Malcolm Orr was one of the crew who joined as a volunteer, and he was the ship's electrical officer, or 'lecky' as they are normally nicknamed. He had started his seafaring career on the P&O liner *Oriana* and had subsequently joined BP. He found joining his first BP tanker, in port in Rotterdam, less than inspiring. Leaving behind the elegance of a P&O liner, he found himself confronted by the rather rusty *British Fern*, nearing the end of discharging her cargo, and, as a result, well down by the stern. Not deterred by this, his next ship was one of the ships that BP had sold to the National Iranian Tanker Corporation. Formerly the *British Surveyor*, she was a VLCC of 215,000 tons and was renamed the *Shoush*. These ships were manned jointly by BP seagoing staff and Iranian nationals. Malcolm Orr joined as the *Shoush* was operating in the Persian Gulf at the time of the Iran–Iraq war. He spent three months in that war zone before requesting a transfer to another ship, while the *Shoush* was in Singapore undergoing repairs. On his return to the United Kingdom he was summoned to BP's head office in London to be questioned on his decision to request a transfer. He explained that he had had enough of being involved in other countries' wars. The response to his comment was to question whether he would he be prepared to be involved in a war where his own country was a protagonist? On conceding that he would, he was advised that he was joining the *British Trent*, which was going to support Operation Corporate in the Falklands. So, after less than two weeks' leave, he joined her in Portsmouth. On 12 April, Easter Monday, he started to keep a diary, which he kept until three days before he left the ship on her return to Portland.

The diary starts after he had spent the night in the Merchant

Navy Hotel at Southampton with much of the remainder of the crew who were joining the *British Trent.*

> The bus to take us to the ship left at about 09.45. Due to hanging about in Southampton for ages, we didn't make the ship until about 11.30... Rob, the lecky [whom he was relieving], showed me around.

They sailed the next day to Fawley on Southampton Water:

> We ... got there at about 1900. While we were sitting there the *QE2* went by. Just like a giant ferry really.

Next day, alongside in Fawley, loading cargo, he:

> spent all morning doing stores. Doubt if we'll sail until about tomorrow morning ... No indication of what's happening yet except that we expect to go to Isle of Grain then back to Portsmouth before we go to Falklands (accompanied by *Intrepid*?).

This guess was correct, as they sailed at 03.15 the next morning, arriving at the Isle of Grain later that day. He found that as there were only two junior engineers on board, he was on watch with the fourth engineer, on the 8 to 12 watch, morning and evening. After the Isle of Grain they returned to Portsmouth, from there proceeding to Portland. On Monday 19 April he records:

> Here we go then!! At anchor all morning at Portland then about noon the bridge received orders. So we left about 12.40. Destination the Ascension Islands. Due on 29 April.

His diary is empty until that date, but then:

> At about 11 o'clock this morning we crossed 7° south into the *'big money'* [the 150 per cent war bonus]. Arrived at Ascension Island at about one o'clock this afternoon. Finally anchored about 16.15. Within minutes, literally, the Royal Navy had the mail on board by helicopter ... There's a lot of ships here, including the *Canberra, Uganda, Elk.* Also a load of RN ships, *Fearless* etc. and the *British Tamar.* Helicopters are everywhere on submarine-search flight

paths. We've got to go to sea in the evening and return to anchor during the day. This is to deter divers apparently. So it means that I'll be on watch again ... How am I expected to do a watch, all of my electrical work *and* that steering gear mod? It's impossible!!

They went out to spend the night at sea, as a security precaution.

On the way out we passed the *Uganda* – what've they done to her? All-white, with red crosses on!! (I really hope that this isn't come to war!!)

The next morning they sailed from Ascension:

So here we are heading south, to some island at about 37° south (six days?). Heavily disguised as a BP tanker heading south. On our own!! A sitting duck! Oh well, at least ... the weather is still nice – so far!!!

On 1 May news of the British air raids on the Falklands was received.

I think I believe the British story – re Vulcans, because we saw them at Ascension.

An element of disenchantment had set in on the next day:

What a dull boring ship this is. This has got to be my last ship! [It wasn't, he stayed with BP for a further period] ... we are a RN ship, number 131 by the way.

On Monday 3 May, news was coming in of other ships that were becoming involved:

Hmmm. So they've taken the *QE2* and two ferries and another container ship, eh? This smells rather strongly of a main landing sometime in the not-too-distant future. News of one of their cruisers being torpedoed is interesting. The trouble is after what we saw at Ascension Island I don't believe all the BBC say. We are due at our rendezvous point tomorrow about 16.00. We'll see what happens then.

Not much did happen for a while. From his diary, one can read frustrations with shipmates surfacing, and the diet changing because of the shortage of stores:

> Wahoo! The ship is slowly running out of stores. The salad stuff is all gone. There is now about two weeks fresh stores remaining. This of course gave B. something else to moan about. He won't appreciate that stuff, especially salad stuff, won't last for ever.

The tensions caused by inactions continued:

> An interesting day ... [A piece of equipment] had a fault on it. I was patiently trying to find this. B. started hassling me and kept on hassling me ... So we are not friends any more, which suits me fine, the more that old Glaswegian bastard stays out of my way the better.

Ten days later, on 14 May, frustration was still in place:

> Still no mail or word of orders. This is getting to everyone, just steaming around at slow speed waiting for orders, mail, or to get attacked. Crew are bored and so are the engineers. The mates haven't seen another ship for about eight days now (if they saw one now I think they'd panic a bit!!) But me, of course, I luv it on here!! Want to go home? Whatever makes you think that?

On 16 May the ship received a message from the Commander in Chief Task Force, which was pinned up for all to read and copied into the diary:

> In accordance with Section 13 of the Naval Discipline Act (1957) a state of Active Service is declared for three months from 0001 GMT on 15 May in the Atlantic Ocean, between 07° south and 60° south for all service [and] civilian personnel. Normal, day-to-day, running of the ship will still be in accordance with the Merchant Shipping Code of Conduct. Purely military decision and NOT political.

Although the fresh stores were running out, BP's reputation for good food at sea was being maintained, although the tensions were still evident:

> Tea tonight was (for me) veg soup, fried hake; spaghetti Italiano (in a cheese sauce). Very nice too!... I'm glad I was brought up to have good table manners, it winds me up to see slovenliness at the table.

Days passed, until on 21 May:

> Well it's *all* happening now. We've finally received orders, we've to proceed straight away at full speed south. Our new holding area is to be around 52° south 50° west. That's just 230 miles off Port Stanley. Oops!! People on board were not *too* impressed.

On the 23rd, a rendezvous with RFA *Pearleaf*, to carry out replenishment at sea (RAS), occurred. Malcolm Orr was not very impressed with her, describing her as a 'tatty looking object'. The RAS ended at 12.30 because of the state of the sea. A fresh attempt was made the next day, and continued through the day from 07.30 until 16.30. It must have been a very smooth operation, the diary comment being 'seems pretty simple, this RAS.' But his comment was a little premature, for on the next day:

> *Pearleaf* RAS'ing again today until she broke down and fell behind. So the lines had to be cut in a hurry. Wahoo! Oil everywhere. I suppose they'll try again tomorrow. More Argentinian planes shot down, eh? And two of our supply ships hit.

Four days later the stores issue surfaced again:

> Tea was good *especially* considering that the stores have nearly run out. There are black bits all over the veg. Fruit is pretty scarce. What there is, is going rotten.

Their next attempt at RAS was with RFA *Olmeda*:

> The rendezvous with *Olmeda* was put back to noon. Then a helicopter started coming back and forward – what a pilot!! Never seen flying like it – brilliant. Don't know about the mail yet – but got some good shots of the chopper ... But the *Olmeda* didn't bother to try RAS. Too rough. It certainly was rough, I never slept a wink (and we're still

bouncing about like a cork!!)

There was no more luck the next day, 1 June, although the helicopters were still flying:

So another month is upon us. There are supposed to be heatwaves at home and we are down here – freezing cold and there was a snowstorm yesterday!! The chopper has gone to *Canberra* to get *Olmeda*'s mail. I wonder if we've got any ... *Olmeda* brought the mail to take north!!! He also accidentally brought *Olmeda*'s mail [to us] – so the pilot will be getting strung up about now.

A few days passed without significant incident. On 5 June he noted:

Stores situation pretty bad. Three weeks linen, one month's potatoes, two weeks' eggs, milk, onion. No fresh veg. One month frozen.

By 7 June sea conditions had eased and RFA *Blue Rover* came to receive ATK (aviation fuel) but 'she's still gonna leave us with approx. 2000 tonnes of ATK so we don't know what's going to happen now.' Two days later they received the news about the attacks on *Sir Tristram*, *Sir Galahad* and HMS *Plymouth*. The following day, the 10th, they learnt that they would take survivors on board for the trip north to Ascension Island. Then they joined the Task Force:

Wow!! Those Harriers landing on *Invincible* – out of this world. We joined the fleet ... in the late morning. Then we took on a helo full of RN guys from *Hermes*. Then we RAS'ed with *Olna*. Tomorrow all the survivors from *Tristram*, *Galahad* etc. will join. Apparently a lot of the Argentinian soldiers taken at Goose Green when told they were on the *Hermes* laughed. They had been told that *Hermes* and *Invincible* were sunk ages ago.

On 12 June, they began to receive their passengers. Extra stores were supplied for the survivors. After storing, the captain put out the announcement 'All operations now complete. The vessel is now under way to Ascension Island.'

A great cheer went up all round the ship. We've got about 90 survivors on board with us, Chinese [crew from RFA ships], RN commandos and RFA survivors from the *Tristram.* The RFA lads are a good bunch ... Tonight in the saloon it was ship's and RN officers first (including SBS and RAF), then second sitting was the rest. This should certainly be an interesting trip. We had a RED this afternoon. (i.e. air attack imminent – Exocet carrying aircraft in the air ... Oh shit!! But they went away luckily).

So they commenced their passage towards Ascension Island. On Sunday 13 June he noted:-

Nine weeks in today. ETA at Ascension Island is a.m. on the 23rd ... Tea was great tonight – especially considering the number of bodies to feed etc. The catering staff are doing *brilliantly* ... It's all good news today – a helicopter is on the way from HMS *Brilliant* with more mail.

A letter from the *British Trent*'s permanent electrician told him that he was rejoining the ship in the UK, so Malcolm Orr would be able to go home on leave. Tension was easing, particularly when the news was received that the Argentinian troops on the Falkland Islands had surrendered. An unexpected benefit was that the Chinese survivors on board were helping in the galley, so Chinese meals were being served in the saloon.

On the next day, they had a thank you message from the CiC Fleet for their efforts. However, four days later:

We received yet another congratulations telegram today. This time from HER MAJESTY THE QUEEN. (Good, eh??)

As they progressed north, the weather improved so that:

Bronzy [sun-tanning weather] has arrived at last! Lovely day, not too hot ... It's like Pontin's up on deck at the minute (but no girls unfortunately). Then we heard what sounded like gunshots. A quick investigation and sure enough it was a gun and an A40 Armalite to be exact. 'Green Death' [SBS commando on board] had to get off 100 shots before Ascension and so he let us shoot off the poop deck at cans etc. Great it was ... I'll never forget the day Clive [a.k.a. Green Death] joined (9 June). I was asleep and heard a helo, so I, bleary eyed, looked out of the window – and saw a marine in full battle dress, gun, the lot, running towards the accommodation. Quite an awakening that. (I thought we'd been boarded).

On 23 June, as expected, they arrived at Ascension Island, where all their passengers left. Sailing the next morning, they were bound for the UK. Four days later they received orders to proceed to Portland, and Malcolm Orr was able to telephone his parents to collect him from there. His diary concludes on 2 July with the words 'no more bronzy and the seas are turning rough.' Clearly the heatwave that he had mentioned earlier had finished.

The *British Trent* arrived in Portland on 4 July, changed some of the crew, reloaded and sailed for Ascension Island on the 12th. She was back in Portland in October but then returned to the Falklands, where she remained until the end of that year.

She continued trading for BP until 1993 when, on 3 June, she was hit by a Panamanian bulk carrier while in the Scheldt estuary, having just disembarked the pilot. In the resulting fire, nine members of the crew died and the ship was completely gutted. She was towed into port and sold for scrap immediately. Having survived the Falklands, it was ironic that she should have met such an end so close to home.

British Tay

The *British Tay* was another of the River class chartered by the Ministry of Defence. At the time her chief engineer was Peter James, who was on board for the first two trips south – and his memories, written down for this book, combined with BP Shipping's record,[2] give a good account of her service.

The *British Tay* was, conveniently, anchored at Swansea when on 5 April she was chartered by the MoD and received

---

[2] BP Shipping Ltd. *Operation Corporate*. London, 1982,14.

orders to proceed to Devonport, where she arrived the next day. She was converted with the appropriate equipment to be able to undertake RAS abeam and, in addition, loaded diesel oil as part of her cargo. While there, the crew were advised about their role, and to ensure they were all willing to volunteer. Only one did not, and he and the apprentices, who were not allowed to sail by BP, left the ship.[3] Three Royal Naval personnel joined the ship, two petty officers to assist with RAS, and a radio officer with a decoding machine. From Plymouth she sailed to Milford Haven and Campbeltown, where she loaded more fuel of different grades, sailing finally from the United Kingdom on 11 April for Ascension Island.

She was the first merchant ship to arrive there, so anchored. She sailed after a few days with all lights blacked out during night time. On arrival at her appointed holding zone, she cruised at slow speed while awaiting instructions to replenish. This she did, with various ships, including RFA *Pearleaf*. By the time they had discharged nearly all their cargo, they were in convoy with various other ships and only 12 miles from the *Atlantic Conveyor* when she was hit by Exocet missiles. Eventually, after rescue and treatment, 133 survivors were transferred to the *British Tay* on 28 May to be taken to Ascension Island. The ship was designed to accommodate a crew of 35, so the trip was very crowded. The crew shared their cabins with the survivors, doubling and in some cases tripling up.

After they left Ascension Island for the second time the ship sailed to the United Kingdom, to reload with three grades of cargo (their original cargo had been aviation fuel, diesel and light fuel oil). She arrived back in the Falklands on 23 July. As the weather was too bad to replenish at sea, she anchored in San Carlos Water and refuelled ships there. In addition to her refuelling activities, she acted as a rest and relaxation ship, and a dental surgery was set up on board in the officers' games room. Dental treatment was provided not only for service personnel, but also to Falkland Islanders. The main beneficiaries of the rest and relaxation were the troops manning the ten

---

[3] As far as it has been possible to ascertain, BP was the only company that did not allow apprentices to be on board for Operation Corporate.

Rapier [anti-aircraft missile] batteries surrounding San Carlos Water who, in rotation, arrived by helicopter for 24 hours rest on the *British Tay*, one man from each battery at a time. Meals were provided for the troops and those attending the dentist. Appreciation of this hospitality was shown by HMS *Birmingham*, who, in the Navy's tradition of quoting the Bible in signals, sent 'see Matthew 25 verse 35' (for I was hungry and you gave me food. I was thirsty and you gave me drink. I was a stranger and you welcomed me).

They sailed for the UK in mid-September. After calling at Ascension Island they had a main engine breakdown, which diverted them, after repairs were carried out, to Las Palmas, where they took spare parts on board. While there, they loaded a Harrier jet that had landed on a container ship, to return it to the UK. The *British Tay* arrived at Portland, where repairs to her engines were undertaken, and then returned to Plymouth to load to return again to the Falkland Islands, sailing on 4 November. She stayed under Ministry of Defence control until the end of 1982.

Eburna

Built in Japan for Shell Tankers, *Eburna* was completed in 1979 with a deadweight of 31,170 tons. She was a motor vessel, with a variable-pitch propeller that could be controlled from the bridge. Like BP's River class, she was designed as a product carrier, with the ability to carry several different grades of cargo at one time. The crew numbered 27 in total, including two cadets, who, unlike in BP, sailed with the ship to the Falklands.

The master, Captain Jack Beaumont, had joined the company after pre-sea training at HMS *Conway*, and he spent his entire seagoing career with Shell, retiring in 1987. By 1982 he had been a master for eight years. His account, which he wrote especially for this book, is reproduced almost in its entirety.

Eburna departed North Shields on 30 March 1982, seen off by my friend, the previous master and his wife. Off the Tyne, we anchored until the evening of 2 April when we heaved up and proceeded to Petit-Couronne to load a full

Canberra in the Falklands, a landing craft alongside.

Another photo of *Canberra*, off Port Stanley, with HMS *Andromeda* 'keeping goal'.

▲ *Uganda* as a hospital ship.

▲ *Atlantic Causeway* in the Falklands.

Atlantic Conveyor, sister ship to *Atlantic Causeway*.

Harrier taking off vertically from the forward flight deck of *Atlantic Conveyor*.

▲ Captains Ian North and Michael Layard (as he then was) on the bridge of *Atlantic Conveyo*

▲ *Atlantic Conveyor*, burned out and adrift in the Southern Ocean after breaking in two following the missile attack.

◄ *British Tay*. It was sunny and hot in the UK!

British Trent at anchor.

◄ Shell tanker *Eburna*. Her funnel was painted black for the war because of Shell's extensive business interests in South America, including Argentina.

Europic Ferry, on her return to Southampton.

St Edmund in more peaceful times.

Stena Seaspread, sister ship to *Stena Inspector*, with HMS *Endurance* alongside.

The tug *Irishman* at work.

RFA *Olmeda*, going south at full speed.

◀ RFA
Sir Lancelot
in a peaceful
moment.

▶
RRS *Bransfield*
in the Antarctic.

▲ *St Edmund* and *Baltic Ferry* lie peacefully at anchor after the war – taken from the bridge
of *Sir Lancelot*.

cargo of gas oil for Hamburg. At Petit-Couronne the phone calls started coming from London head office hinting that *Eburna* could be required for services other than the proposed West Indies charter. All very hush-hush! As though the weather knew more about the future than ourselves, a force 11 gale delayed our passage to Hamburg, where we berthed on 10 April, and sailed the next day. I was informed that we would load an MoD cargo at a port south of a line from Tyne to Clyde. A little outside the limits, we were directed to Invergordon.

By this time all on board had been informed that the vessel was to be chartered to the MoD and the possibility that we could be sent south as far as Gibraltar or Ascension. All hands were given the opportunity to sign off. The main reactions were ... 'I'm not going home in April, I want the summer.' Or the chief engineer's comment that he could not let me go down south on my own! (Little did they know!)

Invergordon introduced us to the delights of non-commercial trading and abbreviations that leave Shell's ... in the amateur status. It is now MODS, RAS, STUFT ... etc. From this time on we were STUFT (ship taken up from trade) and our MoD liaison was to be known as STUFT ONE. Liaison with the shore in Invergordon was excellent although who did the ship's business was a mystery, was it the Shell agency, MoD or RFA? No one seemed to know. Still, apart from my shirt going astray at the laundry, all went very well.

The first shock: cargo will not fit in. Answer: 'but we always work in cubic metres.' Cargo now fits in. Second shock: what temperature do you require the fuel oil to be kept at? Answer: 'just keep it warm.' An RN engineer boarded complete with ship's plans and proceeded to check out modifications needed so that we could carry out the job of replenishment at sea with RFA vessels. Notes and measurements were taken, decisions were made.

The local hostelry made us all welcome and it was generally hoped that the vessel would complete MoD charter running between Invergordon and one of the southern ports. Fuel oil and diesel were loaded and *Eburna* was ordered to Devonport and given an arrival time. Problem: do we slow steam or do we gallop off to make charter speed? Admiral says slow, Shell says gallop. Shell pays wages and has provided last 30 years' training, so we gallop. *Eburna* eventually sailed from Invergordon at 15.00 on the 16th, and I decided to go north about, through the Pentland Firth, in order to cut out the Channel. The passage was excellent and although Paul Jeffery, the Irish second officer, tended to lay off the courses in order to hug the Irish coast, I could find no excuse to favour the Blackpool side of the Irish sea [Blackpool was Captain Beaumont's home town]. The earlier confusion on arrival time repeated itself. You will arrive at Devonport at 14.00 hours 19th. Shell require to keep to charter speed. The captain does not know what the hell to do but as said before, long-term training and chicken attitude gets *Eburna* round in double quick time and nicely anchored off Plymouth Sound for 22.20 hours on the 18th.

Eburna steams gloriously into Devonport, Yonderberry Point amongst happy waving holidaymakers. Possibly they were waving at the tug – she was bigger than us. In fact she was so big that she brought her own mooring gang. We arrived alongside at 15.40 hours on the 19th. What lines for discharge? Only one, for fuel oil. What about the diesel? Not for here, mate. First moment of panic! Barges, workers, stores, one RFA liaison radio officer, one liaison RFA second mate, drums (45 gallons). Question: where are we going? Rumours, we can't say but we think it starts with a G. No Shell personnel on jetty, a phone call for captain: 'sorry we could not get down but my brother will be there to keep an eye on things' (always the brother, never the sister); brother turns out to be a replica of first party, but far nicer personage. The vessel was now fitted out for RAS operations, stored and drummed with no thought to discussions or training of personnel. Quite a lot of problems later encountered could have been solved at this point in time but how were we to know? We did not even know where we were bound.

Orders now received. Sail for Loch Ewe in order to load avcat [aviation fuel] parcel into tanks. We sailed from Devonport at 17.00 hours on the 20th, complete with all new stores. Some items left over from World War II, e.g. lead acid Aldis lamps, charts, flags; MoD must have no knowledge of modern-day MN vessels as our equipment, apart from pairs of Barr and Stroud binoculars, is far superior. It is obvious that a liaison between the MoD and shipping companies in future is necessary in order to keep each other updated. MoD had no idea of modern-day MN ships' equipment and capabilities. A sobering thought when one package loaded contained a huge white flag and Geneva Convention PoW cards. 319 forty-five-gallon drums of lubricating oil and antifreeze were loaded and stowed around the bridge deck (this should have given us a clue!).

The voyage north to Loch Ewe was uneventful and we arrived at 09.00 hours on 22 April. The agent turned up in the form of Blair MacIntyre from London office accompanied by new second officer and petty officer. After partaking of the usual refreshment and completing the ship's business in a very efficient manner (for an engineer!), Blair warned the offsigning second officer and petty officer that he would deliver them to civilisation in his car, but if they were of a nervous disposition perhaps they should wait for a bus, as his driving left a lot to be desired.

Eburna loaded two tanks of avcat and was requested to load a further 400 drums of Castrol lubricants but they were not available at this port. Again the question 'Where for?' No idea but it could start with G or A. Could it be further south? 'Not a chance.' Still be on the safe side better get some cold-weather gear. How many sets? Ten – no, better make it 30 (just as well we did) but might not need them. Yes, but we might. Budgets! We then received orders to proceed to Portsmouth to load 400 more drums and to take on a RFA petty officer. We sailed at 20.00 hours on the same day. Full speed to Portsmouth; an uneventful voyage. We berthed at 14.24 hours on the 25th. A fine view of HMS *Victory* surrounded in scaffolding. A beautiful sight, holidaymakers, pleasure boats, Navy ships, *Victory* and hundreds of those bloody drums! Where do we stand? We are a tanker not a cargo ship.

Departed Portsmouth in the early hours of 26 April, with orders for Curaçao to complete loading navy fuel oil. Heard a rumour that a British vessel would be leaving Portsmouth the bands playing and wives weeping at 08.00 26th. Unfortunately laid on for troopship moored astern of us. Pity! A normal passage to Curaçao except for the main fridges playing up. We arrived on 7 May, and were ordered to fill up with bunkers and fuel oil ... The atmosphere in Curaçao gave the impression of being little strained. Only the top people knew we were loading a MoD cargo and the close proximity to Venezuela with their feelings and embargoes on British ships gave me the feeling that Curaçao officials were little frightened of any involvement that would upset their Venezuelan neighbours. The main fridge was still losing temperature and we requested shore assistance. The vessel delayed until certain of clearing moisture from the system. As there are no shops in the South Atlantic it was not acceptable to leave Curaçao till all was well. For the vessel to be out of commission due to food shortage would have been one for the record, however all was well and vessel fully bunkered, loaded and stored, with fridge system OK sailed at 18.00 hours 8 May.

Our only orders when we sailed were for us to head

east, and it was after 24 hours that we were ordered to Ascension to load mails and stores for the fleet after a 24-hour stopover, but we are only going to start at Ascension so where is this fleet they are talking about? I found out later that the reason we sailed with no orders was to prevent anyone going sick, or writing home and giving away top-secret information. All transmissions to London office and personal messages now cease. Only urgent messages and routine Admiralty messages allowed. Vessels call sign and identity now finished and a daily call sign allocated by Whitehall. Ship's funnel now painted black. Not thought prudent to keep Shell emblem due to large Shell interests in the Argentine. All incoming messages from company now sent through Whitehall and redirected using daily secret code sign. New innovation: a telex machine set up in receive mode using Whitehall frequency. This in effect gave all messages in code and ones for *Eburna* were taken off and decoded on an Enigma decoder. This was done by the RFA radio liaison officer, a good mature operator who knew his way around the decoder and its intricate workings. Some items of the decoder had to be changed daily and others weekly. Messages were difficult to understand with the Navy jargon but again our RFA radio man was well up to this. However the power of the certain department in Shell was soon to become evident when they managed to get through in plain language requesting overtime and victualling figures.

Bad weather all the way to Ascension. Message from admiral asking why we could not make 15 knots as we were required. The vessel was chartered at 14 ¼ knots on summer marks, and we were on tropical marks [i.e. they were carrying more cargo, so were more deeply laden] and we were in adverse weather currents and were performing as well as possible. Southeasterly winds and currents all the way as anticipated. We received two weather forecasts daily from Whitehall for the track we were on, but these forecasts bore no resemblance to the weather we experienced. On 19 May we crossed latitude 7° south. I was informed that this is when the war bonus started, while in truth no one on board had heard of any bonus. We were certainly not there for the money.

On arrival at Ascension we were ordered to anchor ... right in the prohibited area (hope they know what they are up to?). We anchored at 02.00 20 May. No lights allowed ... As ordered by guard ship. Ordered to remain at anchor. During the day two helicopter visits but no mail or stores. Mail sent. Changed films with *British Avon*. A lovely sight to see a Vulcan bomber flying over ... *Eburna* sailed at the appointed hour on the 22nd with no destination. The admiral was reminded of vessel's loaded condition. Vessel ordered south to a ... secret holding area. On arrival 27 May at this secret area, found that we had a company of a Russian spy ship bristling with aerials and scanners etc. Reported this information and we were diverted to a second holding area. We arrived at second area 31 May. On the next day received orders to proceed south on M1 and then west on M4 passing South Georgia en route to a TRALA [tug, repair and logistic area] off Falklands islands. All positions of the route were given.

All drills are going well. The lifeboat painters are left secured to main deck bollards and the drill procedure changed so that the first persons on station commence swinging the boat out, not waiting for the full muster. This, with the added incentive in this part of the world has had the boats swung out and bowsed in at the embarkation deck in a maximum time of 90 seconds. RAS and helicopter drills are well in hand. One idea from the RFA petty officer is that instead of wearing heavy rubber gloves to retrieve the helicopter hook, it would be better to attach a wire and hook to a bamboo pole with a trailing wire shackle, so that the helicopter hook would be earthed as the shackle would be free to slide over the ship's steel deck. [This would prevent the risk of sparks or an electric shock from the helicopter wire, from the build-up of static electricity.] Two areas, one port side and one starboard side (the ship's laundry and crew mess room) were designated for refuge in case of attack. Each space was stocked with tools and first aid items. Officers and crew members were designated to each space, ensuring both deck and engine requirements were covered.

At 15.30 hours on 8 June, in latitude 49° 44.5′ south, we sighted our first iceberg; quite a novelty, and all hands came on deck for a look ... Beautiful. Showed up well on radar. Full moon makes night vision excellent. Although lifeboat engines are run twice daily, fuel lines froze, so had to clear lines and replace oil with naval diesel. No more problems. On the next day, the weather deteriorated rapidly as vessel on westerly course. Force 12 followed by dense fog, speed minimal to avoid icebergs, rain, snow. Up to 30 icebergs showing on 24-mile range on the radar at most times. Four storms of force 12 with winds reaching 80 knots, three days navigating through icebergs, growlers and bergy bits. The barometer is watched closer than the clock. Wind shifts are violent and the seas are mountainous.

Have received word that tanker *British Wye* had been straddled by seven bombs from a Hercules transport plane. One bomb hit the forecastle and bounced off. It seems that we will be the relieving tanker and that the aircraft is looking for us. HMS *Glasgow* diverted to cover our track in case of an attack. Ordered to blackout ship, no radar (except for a quick sweep every few minutes), all navigation lights out; very scary in storms, fog and ice. The westerly route aptly named the M4 had the worst weather conditions that I have ever experienced. We notified the admiral that we were delayed by the weather and ice. He then sent out a general message saying 'ice on motorways' and I believe that southbound vessels including the *QE2* were diverted to another route. [She suffered some structural damage as a result of the weather]. 10 June westerly force 9 all day. [Two days later] clear of ice but gales and fog persist. I have lost count of the number of times that we had to heave to, head to wind, and we quickly learned that dense fog and storms can be present at the same time. Challenged by the guard ship on passing South Georgia. Luckily our coded replies were correct.

At 00.13 hours 14 June arrived at our destination off Falkland Islands, within TRALA, a 5 mile by 10 mile area. Told to take station on a certain ship and keep within 1 mile. Now to sit back and learn the rules of the club!! Chief engineer delighted to be able to top up bunkers from the cargo. Better not try when we return to normal trading. Our first RAS was done during the hours of darkness and it showed how ill-equipped we are with any form of deck lighting. The MoD lights supplied were meant to be plugged in along the main deck. We have no sockets on the main deck. Wrong fittings for anywhere on board, wrong voltage and definitely not intrinsically safe. Could not use our own floodlights because of blackout restrictions. So it was a torch job. We did manage to rig a red light for'd and aft, a wander lead red light at the aft main deck winch and two lights with red-painted glass at the manifold. Semi-inflated lifejackets with auto light were supplied for deck working. Ship's normal lifejackets were far too bulky for working in heavy-weather gear.

The procedure for getting into position for the RAS operation is that *Eburna* steams on a given course and at a given speed. The RFA vessel then closes to within approximately 80 feet. She then fires two lines across, one for'd and one aft. Once retrieved, a rope messenger is passed across, to enable the hose to be winched across and telephone lines are also passed across. The for'd line is used to send across a distance line which consists of a line with chemical lights attached at 5-foot intervals. This is stretched across between the two vessels ... By counting the number of lights, you can see if the distance between the two vessels is fluctuating.

It was a complete disaster. The RFA tanker *Tidepool*, which we transferred oil to, had a lousy connection piece, which eventually fitted the third connection we tried. His valve had to be opened with a sledgehammer and after delivering only 300 tons he had boiler failure and we had to do an emergency breakaway. No blame attached to the RFA vessel, as the vessel concerned had probably been hard-pressed for the last two months, but it did not do our confidence any good. On breaking away from the *Tidepool* he closed us in order to give a slight lee to assist our men on deck. He was light ship [with very little cargo remaining and therefore high out of the water] and we were well down in the water!! Unfortunately, this had an adverse effect and we shipped a heavy sea that washed all of the deck crew off their feet, crashing into pipelines and the after bulkhead. All were recovered safely by our emergency squad, all okay except for one seaman who damaged his ankle. Another RFA tanker, *Olna*, witnessed the incident and was going to launch her helicopter as she thought we had lost our crew overboard. A head count proved that this was not necessary, as all were accounted for.

On the 18th, a doctor boarded by helicopter to check the seaman's ankle. Luckily not broken but badly bruised. Ten per cent of our deck crew out of action. The following day our confidence was restored on our second RAS operation, which was carried out during daylight hours with a very professional vessel, RFA *Olna*. Couplings fitted, valves worked, telephones worked. Once the initial approach and connecting up had been achieved, and after assessing distance keeping and steering the speed of 13 knots with some slight sea and swell and wind ahead 23 knots, I decided to give ASAP automatic steering a try. The reason for this was because with a man on the wheel they tended to pull away slightly from the other vessel, not being used to steaming in such close proximity. I had a lot of confidence with the ASAP as you could set it within how many degrees you wanted to steer depending on the weather ... Even so a seaman was standing close by, ready for instant change-over if necessary. ASAP steered to within 1 degree and was used until final placing of vessels, for breakaway stop. We were complemented by the captain of the RFA tanker on our station keeping and steering. For the next four days we steamed in formation with the elite, the only non-grey vessel on the horizon. Course, speed and zigzags seemed to depend on whether the admiral had had a good day or not. Vessel still blacked out with no lights or radar. 21 June, allowed to use radar but no steaming or other lights. This let us use our digiplot radar. This is excellent for plotting manoeuvres and gives us a check to see if we have coded the course alteration signals correctly.

We received our first mail since Ascension. We have been allowed to send a free radiogram of 30 words each to our families for each two-week period that we are without mail. The cold-weather gear we loaded in UK has been great but not good enough for the bridge. For protection we used our fridge suits but unfortunately although they kept out the cold, they were not waterproof and took a bit of a hammering. A pity we didn't load gloves and sea-boot socks. The officers and crew have been magnificent throughout, carrying out their duties in an excellent manner. What with normal ship routine plus flag hoists, helicopter operations, RAS operations, boat drills, fire drills and air attack drills, all at very short notice. Enough cannot be said about the catering department. They made up a great emergency team and how they managed to keep the good, hot meals coming through all the adverse weather, I just do not know.

At most times between RAS operations, steaming in our designated area with the fleet, we were given lead position in the centre of the group and all and sundry had to keep position on us. No steaming or other lights but now with radar. At intervals, we had to flash an all-round red light to give other vessels a chance of a check bearing. Our two radio officers are having to man radio room and bridge portable tactical radio, working six on and six off. The bridge tactical 'Clansman' radio gives any changes of courses or orders. This is a huge workload so I have made a request to *Hermes* to try and borrow another radio operator.

Our third RAS operation was with RFA *Bayleaf*, and we were to complete all remaining RAS operations with this vessel. This was a perfect operation with a smart and efficient vessel. During the transfer I found out that quite a few vessels were unable to make fresh water. Even on aircraft carrier *Hermes* the crew were using salt water showers. While steaming *Eburna* could make fresh water at no cost and we filled the peak tanks in order to transfer water as well as cargo. On the 24th another RAS with *Bayleaf*. Connected at 07.18 hours. All clear 19.19 hours.[4] Another perfect operation in more moderate conditions. After breakaway we took position as guide ship, steaming within our area.

Sunday 27 June our extra radioman came by helicopter from *Hermes*, a yeoman of signals. He quickly settled in. At lunch it was grilled steak plus five other courses. He thought that this was marvellous and he asked me if we just had one big meal per day. I informed him that this was lunch and that the evening dinner was roast chicken and five other courses. He could not believe it. I think on the

---

[4] This terse comment disguises the fact that the ships were steaming alongside each other, 25 metres apart, for 12 hours, maintaining exact station with each other.

naval ships they were living off one meal per day and Mars Bars. During the day we took part in an anti-submarine exercise. Zigzagging and generally trying to fool the submarine ... All *Hermes* helicopters were airborne with sonar gear suspended below. But the submarine must have sunk half the force without detection, us included. I asked our RFA second officer if the submarine had the same zigzag tables as the rest of the fleet. He replied yes, but he wouldn't use them!! Make your own mind up? Talking of zigzag tables, the Admiralty safes on all British MN ships, which held instructions, all highly secret, on what to do in times of conflict, were not even opened.

On 28 June, weather deteriorating, 08.15 hours connected to *Bayleaf*. Weather poor, wind on starboard beam 25/30 knots. Roll and pitch of both vessels moderate to heavy. Hose at times going like a concertina but station keeping was good under the circumstances. Completed transfer and all clear at 13.20 hours. Weather increasing from southeast. On the 29th vessel rolling heavily in force 11 storm. 21.30 hours for'd main deck drums broke loose. Chief officer and crew on deck to secure. 23.10 hours, drums secure. One man became too attached to one drum and it knocked him off his feet but luckily only bruised. I was getting so fed up of the drums that I asked the captain of *Bayleaf* if he would care to do a swap, but he only had Seacat missiles to offer. I'm sure these drums will still be on board when we return to the UK.

On 2 July the helicopter from *Hermes* came to retrieve their long-lost radio yeoman, but he didn't want to leave because of the conditions and good food he had got used to. However he finally left, with a huge food parcel from the chief steward. It was worth it, as he had greatly assisted with communications and given the two radio officers a little breathing space. *Eburna* steamed up and down with the Task Force in severe weather until 3 July. Zigzags still in operation. On 3 July at 14.00 hours attempted to close with *Bayleaf* but wind and seas too great. Gun line parted and then messenger parted so the RAS was aborted. Wind 13 knots, moderate/heavy swells. All elements 30 degrees on starboard bow. Until 6 July steaming within the area with the fleet. Heavy storms throughout, still zigzagging at night. On 6 July ... wind 20 knots with relative wind astern [so equivalent to] 10 knots. Slight to moderate roll and pitch. Last RAS. *Bayleaf* and then home!

A good last operation with *Bayleaf*. A good friend throughout operations with the Task Force. Had patience with our inexperience, and guided us in making course alterations when zigzagging during the RAS operations. *Eburna* had completed six RAS operations and I feel ship and crew have performed exceptionally well to a very professional and high standard and should be proud of themselves. A last flurry of signals to our Naval friends and off on the voyage home. Due to extreme weather we had to keep the easterly course for quite a while before the sea and swell abated enough to turn onto our northerly course, destination Ascension Island. It is a relief to be able to steam normally with no blacked-out accommodation, full navigation lights and radar. Situation normal. Planned for two days at Ascension, for rest, engine maintenance and fresh stores. Arrived at Ascension and anchored at 06.00 hours on 17 July. During the day, fresh stores arrived by Chinook helicopter – 1100 pounds of beautiful salad and fruit and, to the delight of the chief steward, no invoice. These items were the only products we ran short of. Sailed from Ascension 21.00 hours 18 July bound for UK. Received orders to proceed to Rosyth. En route we made a determined effort to clean up *Eburna* to show her at her best for arrival Rosyth. Communications from London informed us that families and the dignitaries will be greeting us on arrival. Apart from messages and phone calls, the voyage to Rosyth was fairly uneventful but an air of excitement hung around the ship. Anchored off Rosyth 19.39 hours 30 July. Chief cook and catering department working hard in readiness for laying on a buffet for ships company and guests when we berth on the 31st.

Eburna berthed at Rosyth at 12.25 hours on Saturday 31 July 1982 escorted by tugs sending plumes of water into the sky. A rapturous welcome from families and the Royal Scots Dragoon Guards Pipe Band (I found out later that they gave up their day off from the Edinburgh Festival to greet us). A much appreciated gesture. The rear admiral of the port, Shell managing director and office personnel, plus MoD personnel – a wonderful sight, never to be forgotten. I received mail from strangers all over the world, thanking us for our participation in the conflict. Quite a few from places like Gibraltar and the Channel Isles which, however unlikely, could find themselves in the same position as the Falkland Islanders ...

P.S. I always said that we would bring those bloody drums home, and we did!!!

Captain Beaumont concluded by noting that the *Eburna* had a total complement of 30 officers and crew, while the RFA vessels had a complement of over 80. He also noted that the machinery plant ran for 56 days without stopping – which was, as he put it, a bit of a record for a motor vessel. Lastly:

When leaving the Falklands we were asked by the admiral if we had room to take on any extra personnel for repatriation. I informed him that we could take at least fourteen, most with en suite cabins. He didn't believe me, so we carried no extra personnel home.

5

The ferries

Europic Ferry

St Edmund

Europic Ferry

The *Europic Ferry* was a cross-channel ferry operating out of Southampton for Townsend Thoresen Ferries, painted in the distinctive company colours of a bright orange hull with the company name painted in bold letters on both sides. Both before and after her time in the South Atlantic she was employed on the Southampton to Le Havre route as a freight ferry.

The baker's tale

In April 1982 Andrew Flewker was the ship's second cook and baker, and he had become accustomed to the daily routine of the cross-channel ferry. His account was written for this book, and his position in the galley provides yet another perspective on the events of the Falklands War.

I had often wondered why men and women would volunteer to go to war, and I never thought that I would do such a thing, but funny things happen in life and I too was about to get drawn in. In the last few weeks while we had been working, some of the Falklands events had already taken place. The Falkland Islands had been invaded, the *Canberra* was going south and other merchant ships were being STUFT (ships taken up from trade). A rumour was going around that one of our own ferries from Southampton might be going too. That was funny – a cross-channel ferry going that far? Having arrived in port early on the morning of Tuesday 20 April, I was due a few days off, having completed my four day shift. Before leaving the ship the chef gave me a message that I was to pop into the crew office on my way before going home. Whilst I wondered what I had done, the chef joked that they wanted crew to go to war on a ferry! There was no shortage of people who were prepared to go ... so the fact that somebody I knew personally as a friend and workmate had asked me to go, and I knew most of the crew, must have sealed it. My father was not happy; he said it was not my war. I asked my brother, who thought I was mad and now knew I was, not to tell my mother until we had sailed. Some of the crew and officers had been further than the channel ferry routes to the continent and Ireland but some had not. As for myself, I had been deep sea many times …

On Thursday 22 April the headline on the front page of the Southampton Evening Echo read 'Ready for action'. We certainly looked as though we were going further than Ascension, the largest open-top car deck had motorbikes, drums of fuel, the possibility of one or more helicopters arriving later and six 105 mm light guns of the 29th Battery Royal Artillery; the car deck below was full too. Apart from the deep-sea tugs we must have been the smallest Merchant Navy ship in the Task Force, at under 5000 tons. Leaving the port of Southampton we four chefs stood on the afterdeck and only then did I think that I might not see this place again. Then the thought was gone again as a small send-off party on the quay waved us farewell and we went back to work. We had a crew of 40, over 100 soldiers and MoD personnel aboard to cook for. Our next stop would be Portland naval base; we were there for two days while some equipment was fitted … we [then] sailed for Plymouth, where we would meet up with the *Atlantic Conveyor* and proceed to join our escorts.

We have an extra crewman now. He didn't volunteer, he was the night watchman in Portland and fell asleep before going off the ship and woke up halfway up the Channel and he can't get off. And so we settled down and started to get used to our work and find some sort of routine for the day. The galley was towards the forward end of the alley amidships. A door opened into the galley and another door, on the other side, led to the ABs' and engine-room crew cabins and mess room. A service hatch area and counter to the restaurant was where most of our passengers had to queue for their meals. The dining room entrance gave into the forward cross alleyway, the purser's office and more cabins, and a flight of stairs went up to the bar and lounge and more accommodation. One deck up again were the officers' cabins, and the fourth deck was the bridge deck. Our stores were on the car deck one deck down from the galley in two big containers. One was full of beer, vegetables and potatoes and the other, a 20-foot freezer container, was just stacked full of everything right up to the door: frozen chickens, fish, lard, butter, lamb, pork legs, gammons, bacon, frozen vegetables – everything we needed for at least a few months. For the first few days the menu was decided by what was closest to the front until we could get in there properly to find everything.

Working out the menus was not going to be easy. There was a mess room for the ABs and engine room hands but the catering staff had to share theirs with everybody else and it eventually ended up as the video room and for other watch keepers having early meals. As we left the Bay of Biscay the weather improved and the helicopters took to the air. Subsequently meals would be required earlier for their personnel on flying and for deck stations too (which was normal for any watch keepers on 12–4, 4–8, or 8–12 watches). As the baker, my task was to produce enough bread rolls for lunch and enough bread for toast and sandwiches for anyone who wanted, other than mealtimes, on a daily basis until we got home ... Eventually the magic number was 150 rolls and up to twelve two-pound loaves of bread per day. Also I prepared the sweets for lunch and dinner, pastry for pies and then assisted, prepared and served the meals, lunch, dinner and breakfast. Later we were assisted by some Army and RAF lads. They managed all the preparation of vegetables and potatoes, washed up and generally helped out as we were kept busy working a straight shift from early in the morning to eight or nine o'clock in the evening. The evening after this was spent in our or others cabins, as the ship had no crew bar, generally talking about the day's events, what we thought might happen and what we had seen or heard through the day. Our catering accommodation was all two berth, all along the cross alley aft. Ours was on the end of it and the door to the open deck aft was in constant use. Deck and engine crew had single or double cabins with the exception of the bosun, second steward and engine-room store keeper. Their cabins were on the port and starboard sides of the ship. Some were larger than others. Ours was not a larger one, sadly. My six-foot-two companion the assistant cook and I took up most of the room in our approximately 10-foot by 6-foot cabin. If we had visitors the first would usually sit on a bunk and the rest usually had to sit on the deck or stand in the alleyway ...

Our stay in Freetown, Sierra Leone, was no longer than 36 hours. We were berthed stern to stern with the *Atlantic Conveyor* and both our stern doors and ramps were down as MoD personnel moved equipment and stores from ship to ship, as some units were on one ship and their equipment was on another. The *Norland* was also berthed alongside; some of the troops on board our ship had their gear on the *Norland*, because to avoid union action in Hull the ship was moved to Southampton with their equipment before they got there. There was also a rumour that the day before they arrived, soldiers had been having gunnery practice with rifles or machine guns and one of them had shot what he thought was a seagull but according to the crew it was an albatross. Merchant seamen are known to be superstitious and this act would have been believed to have brought bad luck to crew and ship ... They demanded that the person responsible be removed before the ship sailed or there would be a strike, but all must have been resolved because we all sailed together.

Between Freetown and Ascension Island the 'crossing the equator' ceremony was held. The galley staff were only too pleased to come up with a recipe of slime for the occasion, mainly comprising flour, water, eggs and food colouring which would be daubed over their bodies. It was probably the last bit of fun to take place on board, as the events that took place just prior to our arrival at Freetown have changed the cabin discussions in the evening. News that a Vulcan bomber has taken off from Ascension and bombed Port Stanley airfield, a 200-mile exclusion zone has been put into place around the islands, and that the *Belgrano* has been sunk, has now really changed the thoughts of all on board. Our hope that we would only go to Ascension and that the politicians might solve this diplomatically has gone. Now we all knew retaliation would come, but how and when was part of the game of war.

We heard the news of the attack on the *Sheffield* on 4 May, when the news came that she had been struck by an Exocet missile. Many had been killed or injured and they had been rescued before the ship sank. I asked someone what one was and I was told that it was a heat-seeking missile and would lock onto its target by size, largest first. 'Heat-seeking meaning the engine room?' I asked. 'Yes, and the galley,' was the reply. We had had a walk around the car deck, and judging by the amount of pallets of ammunition, equipment for 2 Para, snow cats and lots of other suspicious-looking green and brown crates, if we were hit we would make one hell of a bang ...

I had been to Ascension Island before, we used to be the only link to Africa and the UK and I never saw another ship there ... There was no port, everything was craned off onto floating pontoons powered by converted bulldozers and taken ashore to a jetty. When we arrived early in the morning of 7 May and joined the other ships that were anchored off the island, the air was full of helicopters and there was no doubt we were now going to war, something we did not really want to think about or experience but there was no going back for any of us now ... morale was brilliant. We sailed the same evening with the Amphibious Task Group. Everything has changed yet again as we now head south joined with the Carrier Battle Group. The whole ship's crew has been split into two teams, enabling a 24-hour watch with half the crew being stood down whilst the other continue their duties. As *Europic Ferry* steamed south, the measures for defence and action stations were put up on the notice board:

Defence stations: come into force in an area of possible attack. The ship's company will operate as two separate watches. The bridge will be double-manned with engine room in a standby condition. Due to round-the-clock working a continuous light meal service will operate. A steward not required for the meal service will operate a patrol around the accommodation. Individual stations will be allocated by heads of department.

Action stations: come into force in an area of probable attack. The whole ship's company will be up, and the damage control teams closed up. In general, refreshments will be bought to stations by the stewards, except for the engineering department who for practical reasons will eat in their mess. Again the catering department will provide a roving patrol to spot anything unusual. An action stations bill is being made out. Blowpipe teams will stand to and be available at instant readiness. Any further defence measures will be announced. The introduction of defence stations will be announced in advance. The signal for action stations will be the intermittent ringing of the alarm bells.

For the assistant cook and me that meant we would now work from 10 p.m. until 10 a.m. the following day, which was not a problem. What was a problem was that our cabin porthole looked straight out onto what was now an operational flight deck for helicopters all day. So what with the tannoy in the alleyway announcing 'incoming flights' and 'hands to flying stations', the banging of the door against our cabin bulkhead wall as people went to and from the outer deck, not much time was spent sleeping. We had already experienced that sleep in the afternoon was impossible. To be asleep when the alarm bells did go off was frightening enough ... So we got used to having a few beers, listening to some music and playing cribbage until it got too dark to fly any more, usually about teatime, and then we could finally get some sleep (with one eye and one ear open, just in case!).

We had already had a lifeboat drill, the catering department as usual making up the first aid team, and we all had our little jobs to do like collecting the stretcher and first aid kits, securing the galley by making sure everything was safe to be left indefinitely (pots and pans move at sea). My job with the assistant cook was to go outside and up onto the bridge deck where, behind the bridge, were two big air vent doors (more like big windows) that allowed the heat from the galley to escape, and these had to be closed and secured by two lugs. This would shut out any light that would otherwise be visible. They also had to be closed in rough weather. Having done that we could then return to our muster station, which was at the central stairway in the cross alley forward where there were exit doors to the port and starboard sides of the ship and access down the alleyways in the crew accommodation to the after deck.

On one occasion ... our captain had flown to the *Atlantic Conveyor* for the afternoon with some other personnel, the weather was ... at least gale force 8 or 9 and a boat drill was called. So, as normal, we proceeded with our drill, which at that time was first to muster in the galley with our bags of thermals and adequate clothing.

This was as much as you could get on, because the water and the weather was freezing, so to protect oneself from hypothermia you had to don as much clothing as possible. In my case it was thermal socks, leggings and long-sleeved sweatshirt, checks [cook's uniform] and a jacket, then my jeans and another pair of socks, then my wellies, my coat and souwester and finally a lifejacket. In a waterproof bag we put our valuables and seaman's ID book in case we got taken prisoner. The vents were shut and we were all in the galley looking at each other and talking, waiting for the next tannoy announcement, and when it came it was a shocker. I remember the look on their faces when the words 'Attention! This is not a drill' came out of the tannoy. We were to ... go to the restaurant immediately ... The cook and his assistant were not tall and thin to say the least ... And now we had to get out of the galley, which was a bit of a squeeze ... J. and I decided that actually the quickest route was over the hot counter service area into the restaurant, so with a little run and jump we bounced off the counter and onto the floor. We sat around for a while and took off our lifejackets. There was thought to be a submarine in the area, the thought of which was scary, not that we would know much about it ... not with the amount of ammunition we were carrying. I remember one or two people wanting to look out of the port and see if they could see it. They would have been lucky to see us, as I'm sure we spent more time under the waves than above them. At times the weather was just like the North Atlantic winter only worse, and this was one of them. Then we had to lie on the deck – 'apparently the safest position to be in when threatened with a torpedo is lying on the deck with your bum in the air' someone had said in a quiet moment. The cook was more worried about the roasties in the oven going brown, and that brought another sigh: oh no, not the roasties!

On 16 May we joined the rest of the British Task Force.

I was out on deck on a rare occasion when there was no flying, so I had walked to the end of the ship and gazed at the horizon. I heard an aeroplane approaching, it got bigger and then it was gone, a great big Russian spy plane. I wondered whose side they were on.

At 10 o'clock in the evening of 20 May our longest day had just begun. We were all blacked out, ports and deadlights down and at the end of each alleyway aft when you stepped outside onto the deck, you had to close the door behind before you lifted up the tarpaulin cover and stepped into total darkness on the outer deck. As we steamed towards our destination, there was a clear sky and lots of stars. After a few minutes you could focus properly and see the silhouettes of the other ships as we moved towards San Carlos Bay. The only ship we could not spot was the *Canberra*, who soon slowly appeared on the far horizon behind us, her mast all lit up like a Christmas tree, and then it went dark again. Creeping in, we hoped undetected, into Falkland Sound, towards San Carlos Bay.

As we passed Fanning Head tracers could be seen as light arms fire was taking place, and we returned to our duties in the galley. As we got used to the light again, the alleyway was full, all the troops had now been issued with their live ammunition and they were preparing to be taken ashore to the beachhead in San Carlos Water. I don't think I was as frightened as them, but I was scared of the unknown or the obvious (like what happens when the sun comes up?). We had just spent the last six weeks [*sic*] getting to know some of the lads and now it was time to do what we came down here for. I felt sorry for the soldiers who had just been informed that they would be leaving the ship soon and would meet up with the rest of their units later that morning. Poor buggers, it's so cold, it's not a time to go to the beach, I remember thinking.

A few hours later, at breakfast time on that day, 21 May, the clouds went away early, the sun came up and we could see all the way down the bay. The sky was blue, not a cloud to be seen, and looking at the *Canberra* you would have thought she was on a cruise, but the other ships would have told another story: *Fearless, Norland, Intrepid, Stromness, Canberra, Fort Austin, Sir Galahad, Sir Geraint, Sir Lancelot, Sir Percivale, Sir Tristram*. The air was alive with helicopters lifting nets of stores and ammunition ashore to the beachhead whilst the soldiers were being ferried from the ships to shore. It was a hive of activity. We were still painted in our brilliant orange with big white letters painted all the way down the side that read 'Townsend Thoreson'!

The first alarm of incoming aircraft came about 10 o'clock in the morning ... The sound of the *Fearless* and *Intrepid* ships' horns sounding out around the bay sent us both rushing for the top deck to close the vents above the galley (they had been opened to release the heat). It all happened really quickly – up one flight of stairs, then the second, up to the bridge deck. Looking around we could hear the planes and suddenly there they were. They looked like they were coming straight at us as we slammed down the vent covers. The soldier ... on top of the bridge housing opened fire with his mounted machine gun, shouting rude words, as we ran for cover behind a container on the bridge. The noise was excruciatingly loud as the planes flew past and we headed down the other stairs to the main deck again where soldiers were lined up ... firing at the fast disappearing aircraft running the gauntlet of the other ships firing at them. We sat on the stairs for a while as we were obviously not allowed ... nor did we want to go out there anyway. Each time aircraft came in the soldiers would run out onto the deck, fire at them as they approached and then run through to the other side to fire again. I don't think they hit anything but they made it very difficult for the enemy pilots ... I did see a plane get chased by a Sidewinder [missile], the poor pilot managed to eject as his plane exploded and a great cheer went up and then a little silence as the pilot hit the hillside: I don't think he survived.

They were so low at times it was incredible. One bomb exploded between us and *Intrepid* and we really did think *Canberra* was going to be hit but thankfully it fell short, making a big splash in the water very close to her after end ... All day they came, crisscrossing the bay, two, three, four and five at a time. We had been told that the Rapier missile system was to be set up and that would enable them to pick off the enemy aircraft. The rest of us who were not working had turned to on the deck below and we helped load the nets for the helicopters as they hovered above the stern ramp, or loaded the Mexeflotes [self-propelled pontoons] throughout the rest of the day. Nobody took shelter, we just carried on with our job. We were so utterly exhausted, I *think* I had a beer and went straight to bed, having to turn out again at 10 p.m. Several bombs had hit their target and failed to explode. *Ardent* and *Antelope* had taken on board unexploded bombs and brave men were fighting against time to make these safe, but sadly they failed.

Everyone knew on 25 May there was a greater risk of being attacked, as it was Argentina's national day. We were already at action stations as the alarm had been raised for aircraft attack. We were closed up with our escorts, changing our positions regularly and with the *Atlantic Conveyor* moving into our last position. We were heading to San Carlos Bay again to unload more badly needed supplies and equipment. A merchant ship had been hit and we went out onto the deck to see what was going on. I cannot describe the sadness we felt, now standing on the deck with fellow officers, crew and soldiers watching the smoke billow from the *Atlantic Conveyor*. We had sailed all the way from home with her and now she would go no further. Severely damaged, abandoned and taken in tow, she sank later the next day.[1] There was anger that we had guessed correctly. At the time the Exocet picked out the largest target, *Hermes*, which put up chaff to protect herself. This deflected the oncoming missile and so it locked onto the second biggest target, which was unarmed and had no defences ... Some of us knew crewmen on board. I had sailed with the bosun, and the captain I knew from my Port Line and Cunard days ... We didn't know how many casualties there were until later on.

We proceeded to San Carlos Bay again to unload ... After discharging those stores we were sent to a safe zone or holding area until we were required again, leaving just to go around in grid-mapped squares in a holding area somewhere south of the Falklands for nearly a week ... Along with other ships who were refuelling at sea, and others taking on or off stores. Watching a RAS at sea was very interesting. The RFA store ship was running alongside ... as, with the aid of winches, pipes were passed over and connected to us as we took on oil and fresh water ... We had mail deliveries and collections too. We had had plenty of time to write letters home but there was little to write about and there were only certain things you could write ...

The loss of the *Conveyor* had serious setbacks for the ground troops, especially the loss of the Chinook helicopters. As we were equipped with a helicopter landing deck we were dispatched to rendezvous with the *Contender Bezant* somewhere at sea, so that two Chinooks were flown onto our deck with the intention of them ... being flown to another vessel later. This was delayed as we had to battle with force 10 and 11 gale conditions with some monstrous waves reaching between 40 and 50 feet

---

[1] She did not in fact sink until 28 May. See the account in Chapter 6.

high.[2] On one occasion the bridge was flooded by a huge wave which we hit in the middle of the night, frightening the lot of us who were up (thoughts of torpedoes) and causing a few to wake up as the bang reverberated throughout the ship. If it had continued I think the helicopters would have been pushed over the side for our own safety, however the weather had eased by morning and they were able to fly off later the next day.

A day or two later we heard that the war was over and the Argentinians had surrendered. It came as a relief to all of us as we were ordered to Port Stanley ... The area had supposedly been cleared of mines and we proceeded to the inner harbour, where we remained transferring more equipment, stores and personnel. One morning ... I was able to go ashore by launch and take some mail to an office in Port Stanley. It was a small place, cold, with smoking buildings, and soldiers everywhere. I saw some of the Argentinian soldiers who had surrendered, who looked tired, cold and hungry and very young. I found the office and then made my way back to the ship ...

We sailed for home on 23 June. The journey home was really boring. For some reason we in the galley were kept on the night shift all the way home ... I can't remember giving any thought to what I might do when we got home or where we would go, until we arrived off the Channel. We anchored off Plymouth, where a few people joined the ship, including our purser who had been flown home sick, some press, who we were not allowed to talk to (!) and a few other important people from the company and MoD. We steamed up the Channel that evening, and early the next morning, after breakfast, we entered the Solent off the Needles and were soon greeted by little boats, yachts and pleasure craft that cheered and waved as we passed.

---

[2] This was corroborated in Captain W J C Clarke's account as master, in D G Fletcher Roberts, *Conways and the Falklands*, Dunstable, 1983.

The closer we got, the more appeared and, looking through a borrowed pair of binoculars ... I noticed my brother and mother waving frantically ... We were greeted by hundreds of friends and families on the quayside and a few hours later the voyage was complete when we signed off and left the vessel.

St Edmund

Completed at Cammell Laird's yard in Birkenhead in 1973, the *St Edmund* was constructed for Sealink Ferries and was 130 metres long, with a beam of 22 metres. To aid manoeuvrability, she had two variable-pitch propellers, each of which was powered by two diesel engines.

For some five years before the Falklands War, she had been employed on the Harwich to Hook of Holland route. In accordance with Sealink practice, all her deck officers had Foreign Going Masters Certificates. As was often the case on ferries, her crew were generally more mature than those on deep-sea ships – family men, who worked a 24 hour on 24 hour off pattern, they enjoyed that fixed work system which allowed them regular time at home with their families. They were all required to live within easy reach of Harwich.

She was not taken up from trade until May 1982, and by the time she arrived at the Falklands the hostilities had ceased. Her master for the voyage south was Captain M Stockman, who has died since that time. The crew that went with him all thought that they would only get as far as Ascension Island before returning, but they and the troops they had on board carried on and arrived at the Falklands, where the ship stayed until February 1985. Volunteers among the officers were not numerous, but because of the deteriorating state of the Merchant Navy, with redundancies being widespread at all levels, the crew all volunteered. They had a preference for being paid, but being in the Falklands was only marginally preferable to being unemployed.

So in May 1982 she sailed from Harwich and arrived in Devonport, where two helicopter flight decks were fitted, and, among other modifications, her four diesel engines were tuned to run on marine diesel rather than the heavy fuel oil that they normally used. The bow doors were welded shut; this was as a safety precaution against the seas of the South Atlantic. The volunteer crew did not join until the works had been completed, having taken the train from their homes in Harwich down to Plymouth. The crew were immediately struck by the changes that they found in the ship.

The second officer's diary

Louis Roskell was one of three second officers on the St Edmund, and he kept a detailed diary at the time. He was an experienced ferry officer, as he had been sailing on ferries of various types for twelve years before 1982, and had spent a good part of that time crossing the North Sea from Harwich to the Hook of Holland. The route suited him because he was at home regularly and was able to have a relatively normal family life with his wife and two sons. His settled routine changed on 13 May when he was told he would be joining the St Edmund to sail for the South Atlantic. On Sunday the 16th they went by train from Dovercourt to Devonport, from where coaches took them to the Naval Dockyard. Their first view of the St Edmund came as a shock:

> We were, I suppose, prepared for surprises but, even so, our first sight of the St Edmund was a shock. She appeared as though she was being rebuilt. Two helicopter platforms, masses of wiring, strengthening and men everywhere. The noise and confusion was terrific. The mainmast had gone, the bow door welded shut, spark's [radio officer] cabin was now an extra radio room ... then we went for a look at the bridge. Again, men everywhere; new equipment: satnav, heavy-duty windscreen wipers, wires and gear everywhere, panels down ... Some crew arrived late and were obviously under the weather, attracting the scornful looks of the dockworkers and naval staff.

Having spent many years on short sea ferry routes, his

navigation skills were a little rusty for long passages, so he
went:

> ... to Plymouth Nautical College for a crash (revision)
> course in navigation. The lecturer was very kind, having us
> on our own in the classroom and filling us full of
> knowledge. How much there was to remember! Even all
> the tricky bits of taking an error and, as for Captain Marcq
> St Hilaire – well never mind.[3]

They sailed out of the dockyard on 19 May for exercises at sea.
As he had been on the midnight to 4 watch:

> I arose about 0745 and had breakfast shortly afterwards.
> By this time we were well out at sea and heading for our
> rendezvous with *Grey Rover*, our RFA replenishment
> tanker ... at 1015 the first ever RAS (replenishment at sea)
> took place between a Sealink ferry and an RFA. It was an
> amazing sight for one who has only seen it on television.
> The two ships, steaming parallel, only 120 feet apart: the
> bows of the *Grey Rover* lifting slightly with the swell and
> the captain and mate working to maintain speed and
> position. During the RAS, which, due to pumping difficulty,
> took about three hours, I hung up all the boat station lists
> on which I had been working. During the afternoon, we
> returned to Plymouth and went through the range to test
> our degaussing,[4] doing Williamson turns[5] at each end of
> the manoeuvre.
>
> We had hardly touched alongside at Devonport before
> embarkation; the troops were already waiting on the quay.
> I did not go ashore, and found myself busy chasing up
> stores and actually succeeded in locating two sextants ...

---

[3] Captain Marcq St Hilaire developed the method of using star sights to fix a ship's
position.

[4] Degaussing neutralises the magnetic field of the ship to protect it from magnetic
mines.

[5] The Williamson turn, developed by an American naval officer, enables a ship, after
changing course by 180 degrees, to be on the same track as before. It is of particular
importance when searching for a man lost overboard.

At 20.02, as we swung off the quay and headed down towards the narrows, we sounded three long blasts. People on the quay cheered and even the chain ferry flashed his lights and blew his siren. A little further downstream people were cheering and waving and one girl in the group of three lifted her skirt and gave us all a flash. What a morale booster! ... It was something of an anticlimax when we anchored for the night in full view of the town.

They eventually sailed from Plymouth Sound on 21 May. On the following day his afternoon watch was quite busy:

During lunch, heli-ops started between us and the [*Contender*] *Bezant* and I had my first spell as OOW [officer of the watch] bringing the ship head to wind, reducing speed, etc. A busy watch in fact and 16.00 soon came round.

More heli-ops with the *Contender Bezant* followed over the next two days, culminating with a RAS trial:

At dinnertime, we did a RAS trial with *Bezant*. Again it was an interesting sight to see and even hear the other ship so close. One could see her bulbous bow lifting and breaking gently with the foam moving in a measured broken stream between us. We did not receive her line, probably due to a fault with the setting of her gas cartridge, but the trial was a success. I was again off watch, so I stood on the funnel deck [to observe].

On 28 May they arrived at Freetown, in Sierra Leone, West Africa, to take bunkers. Their arrival was not a complete success:

Dreadful tie-up, moored alongside *Contender Bezant*. Her crew had as much idea of seamanship as Auntie Lottie. Hot and humid; no mail – never mind. I shall call them the 'Bezantines' ... As far as I can tell, the stop in Freetown was a complete and utter waste of time. Our call was to take bunkers and this could have been successfully achieved by barge but, on instructions, we went alongside *Bezant* at the Kissy Fuel Oil Jetty and lay all morning without connecting up. It was incredibly hot and humid and we sweated it out until 4 p.m. before they even got a hose to us. When they finally connected up the oil wouldn't flow under gravity! However, we took some stores and sailed regardless at about 20.00. Later, we discovered that all the flour embarked was weevil-infested and so it was thrown overboard ... By the time I came on watch, we were well out to sea. The watch was a warm one, with rainstorms all round us and frequent livid flashes of silent lightning.

The diary entry for the next day is headlined 'ARTICLES OF WAR 2282 DISPLAYED'. However, other matters occupied their minds that day:

During the morning, preparations were underway for the visit of King Neptune, due to make his appearance at 2 p.m. ... I slowed down the ship at the order from King Neptune, then, as we resumed our passage, the celebrations duly began. Captain Stockman appeared ready to be taken like a lamb to the slaughter, dressed in pale blue shirt, shorts, hat and shoulder straps. I performed the usual second mate's task of dodging rain squalls so as not to spoil the ceremony. Then at about 14.45, an act of treachery. Captain Stockman relieved me on the bridge and I was taken by the bears to King Neptune, duly dressed in his rope yarn beard, complete with trident, and shamefully dowsed in the horrible mixture they had prepared. Not so much a ducking, more a biological soak, you might say, which is where my uniform is now – in soak.

The revision course in navigation had clearly been of benefit:

Have I mentioned navigation? The satnav is a marvellous little box of tricks and gives us a constant updated DR [dead reckoning] position obtained from sat fixes. Naturally, we are also taking sights and it is quite surprising how it all comes back. Alistair has taken on the official designation of navigator and, assisted by Bill in the forenoon watch, works sun sights and distances etc. I just take a sight in the afternoon to keep my hand in. I 'm a dab hand at compass errors now, and beginning to learn the stars again.

They arrived at Ascension Island on 31 May. As the ship was blacked out at night, when he awoke at 08.15 he could not see the island until he went to the bridge:

The first impression of the island viewed suddenly, from an anchorage, was strangeness. Everything was brilliant in the sunlight and totally different in view and atmosphere from the sea environment of the last day or so. We were lying alongside the large rubber fenders of the tanker *Alvega*, and both ships were ranging and bumping in the swell. The sea, whisked by a fresh offshore breeze, was a bright unreal blue with white caps. Ascension Island could be seen easily from one end to the other as we lay in the Northwestern Anchorage off Clarence Bay, and its lower slopes were brown and black, in various shades (if you can have shades of black). Humps and bumps, conical and rounded, with buildings dotted here and there. Shadows passing across the surface of the island causing a constantly changing pattern, and high above the highest point of Green Mountain had its permanent cap of orographic cloud swirling turbulently, occasionally shrouding the higher buildings in the mist and, presumably, providing a very localised shower of rain from time to time, on the windward side. Through the binoculars, a view of the little settlement complete with church, clock tower etc., unnaturally bright with trade wind sunshine.

I mentioned that we were rolling and ranging alongside the tanker, but I was surprised to see that we only had the flimsy head wires out and they were alternately hanging slack, then coming up with a singing jolt as the two ships rolled away from each other ... Soon, I couldn't resist it, and I was down on the foredeck ranging out a second wire [while] at the same time we had to drop astern to line up our bunkering position. What a hair-raising business, with the wires grinding and singing all over the place. As the morning went on, things became more and more frantic, with barge and helicopter activity, and at the same time the bridge seemed to fill up with semi-official personnel. Wires came under even more strain as the swell began to increase and eventually, whilst I was having lunch, they began to break ... in fairly rapid order and then we had to start bow thrust and engines to keep her alongside. Thankfully, we completed bunkering at about 13.00 and to cries of 'good luck' from the tanker crew, moved out to our anchorage position.

In the afternoon Louis Roskell had to take one of the boats away to collect personnel from the shore. The boat work continued into the evening but he was back on the bridge for midnight. As was the rule, at Ascension Island the ships left the anchorage at night. The *St Edmund* made use of this time:

... so that we can make fresh water. Our consumption is enormous with so many people on board and baking in such heat. Our tanks are only designed to last 24 hours so the problem is intense. We have two 'osmosis' plants and each plant can make five tons per hour. The man who looks after these plants ... is a VIP on this ship. Sixteen miles off Ascension, we have stopped engines and are drifting, while our osmosis plant works away at making fresh water. There is none to spare, of course, on the island, otherwise we wouldn't be doing this.

Back at the anchorage, the next morning they exercised all their lifeboats and in the afternoon they took some troops with their equipment to the *Tor Caledonia*, with:

... an incident I would have been happy to forget. The trip was a long one, and we were laden down with soldiers and ammunition, including missiles and launchers. When we arrived at this high-freeboard vessel, there were no boat ropes rigged and I refused to take her in until they had provided two ropes, decently spaced. We made it alongside and disembarked the soldiers, but they wouldn't accept the gear unless we went to the stern ramp. This was highly dangerous, with her stern rising and falling up to 6 feet with the swell and the ramp threatening at any time to catch our boat underneath and crush it. We tried to get alongside by driving the boat alternately ahead and astern (mainly astern) and getting nowhere. In the end, I was forced to take over myself and we went in at full pelt, made fast on long lines and, with everyone fending off, threw the gear onto the stern ramp. What a dangerous business. One minute the ramp was buried in a welter of foam and the next it was high out of the water. All this, with the noise of the engine drowning all conversation.

On this ship, as has been seen on some others, the prospect of proximity to a war zone affected some members of the crew:

A young AB on my watch has been sent home – no sleep, frightened etc., all rather sad. Also, today, the NAAFI manager tried to run away, but was apprehended at the airstrip, trying to hitch a lift home in a Hercules. It really doesn't pay to remember all those stories about people's premonitions, does it? One could be scared to death. Writing about it gives me the jitters, and I can imagine these two incidents being singled out in the future, as an example of how people foretold a disaster.

They sailed on 3 June, continuing their journey southwards. The weather continued to be settled:

The weather was still warm and sunny ... But now, from the south, is coming a long, long swell and the ship so far is handling it very well. Most of us feel that, if we had been in shorter seas such as in the North Sea, she would have been thumping and shipping spray, but here she is dancing along, rising majestically on her toes then sinking gently before steadying up and repeating the performance ... The ship is now very crowded, with camp beds everywhere, even in the ladies' lavatories. The second-class bar is a dormitory, with camp beds and kit everywhere. This is because of all the extra personnel embarked at Ascension. The car deck is fairly full of gear, including in the lower part our plant for making fresh water: there are also containers containing the frozen food and quite sizeable 'pens' containing dry goods. The dreadful smell coming up the lift shaft has now been seen to come from the potatoes, stowed in the heat of the car deck, but when I went down this morning they were being moved onto the open deck.

Three days later, on Sunday 6 June, the differences between the Royal Navy and the Merchant Navy came to the fore:

Inter-service rivalry: it exists, obviously, between airmen, soldiers and sailors. It exists between units of the same service, it exists on this ship. With regard to our relationship with the Navy, it is slowly changing. Changing, not deteriorating, however. At the beginning of our voyage, we were somewhat in awe – at least, I was; their discipline and training, their obvious confidence, backed by a certain consideration for our somewhat 'quaint' practices, caused us to give them the benefit of the doubt in any question of judgement. Being under naval control also caused us to accept more or less everything they imposed. 'Give an inch and they take a mile' might have been coined for this ship, because, more and more, the first lieutenant has been picking up control of our emergency stations and imposing his own ideas. For example, the implementation of action stations (necessary), the herding of crew into assembly stations (madness), the abandonment of lifeboat davit positions so that every life raft would be thrown over the wall (madness in Antarctic conditions) ... This morning, however, Captain Stockman finally said 'enough' and has taken over the emergency planning and drills himself ... It says something about our poor organisation, but you realise we are three weeks into the voyage and we are still changing routines ... The smell of rotting vegetables now permeates the ship as our inexperienced stewards have been storing the stuff in 90 °F temperatures on the car deck.

The next day the weather changed for the worse:

At 18.00 a dramatic change in the wind direction to the south, and it increased to force 10. Looking forward from the bridge, it was a real classic, with a grey, angry misty succession of foaming waves. Soon we were pitching heavily and hove to, as the succession of very large swells passed under us. The noise was terrific and the storm hit with such suddenness and ferocity, that our air-defence soldiers were still on the funnel deck and had to be brought down only after being soaked with the torrential rain which was driving almost horizontally by this time.

On 10 June he went on watch at midnight, to be given the news of the attacks on the *Sir Galahad* and the *Sir Tristram*. He commented in his diary:

Yes, the news is very bad, from the Falklands. I feel that I am now committed to going through a very difficult time. Three ships have been sunk, and this has been a real victory for the Argentinians. The loss of life must be measured in hundreds, and of course everyone is wondering if that will be our fate also. Looking around my fellow crew members, I can read all sorts of things written on their faces. Things look so bad now and we shall be there on Monday. Of course there's nothing we can do about it – we certainly can't turn back but must now see it through to the end.

On the 15th, however, they heard the confirmation of the surrender of Argentine land forces on the Falkland Islands. Their progress to their destination was slowed by more bad weather:

Unfortunately with our need to get to the area as urgent as ever, we are frustrated by the weather once again. Not just a gale, but a storm force 11 from the south with 40-foot-high waves and driving snow. We had no alternative, in view of the Chinooks assembled on the stern of *Europic Ferry* and *Bezant*, to run before this wind to the nor'd. About halfway through the watch, with steering very difficult, the AB put the helm over the wrong way and we broached to, amid all the sounds of breaking equipment and sliding gear. We lay further and further over, as I took the wheel from him and forced it hard a port. Frantic, I got the engineer to give me a third engine (it was all they had, number four was having a minor repair). We slowly recovered and were back on course in what I suppose was a minute or two but seemed ages ...

We thought the storm wouldn't last but it continued unabated all day, and by the afternoon we had turned and were running into it. The movement and wind strength have proved too much for the Chinooks and one ... bladed up and ready to go has been severely damaged ... The 12–4 p.m. watch was very spectacular, particularly in the squalls, when the sleet blows almost horizontal. At times we are rolling so much that the stabilisers come out of the water! Things became even worse during the evening, and my cabin was a mess, with all my drawers shot out across the cabin floor. No sleep at all, then on watch at midnight.

Despite the weather, activity became much greater the next day:

The p.m. watch was one of our busiest, with practically continuous air ops. I managed to get a tape-recording of parts of it and it sounds really chaotic. The first part was spent steaming apparently aimlessly up and down wind in the TRALA [tug, repair and logistics area], following first one ship then another. So many alterations of course were flying around and the sea conditions were so difficult, that at one time we seemed to be steaming towards each other – all of us heading for one central point. The noise on the bridge was tremendous and at times it took on an atmosphere of unreality. Eventually, an order came for us to proceed to a rendezvous position and 'suspend present operations'. As one we all turned onto a course of 250 degrees and closed up. *Brilliant* inquired our probable speed under present weather conditions, which were rough, but not nearly as bad as of late, so I said we could easily do 17 knots. She then ordered us to 'proceed at best speed, you are guide.' ... Soon we were up to 19½ knots and heading up. The *Bezant* dropped well behind and we were gaining on the *Brilliant* when we were told to hold back and formate [*sic*] on *Bezant* yet again. Yet we had had our moment of glory – we had shown what we could do. Instead of wallowing, the stabilisers had begun to bite and one could actually feel the morale of the ship rise with the whine of the turbo blowers as we steadied up and started to build up towards our maximum speed. She was as steady as a rock, with just the odd tremble, as we sliced the top of the swell. Never mind.

On 17 June they arrived at Port Stanley:

The captain let me con the ship through the narrows and into the anchorage actually off the town of Port Stanley. By this time, we were so busy with heli-ops that one even landed on as we were coming through the narrows. [Later in the day] President Galtieri has been deposed – new hardliner now in command of military junta. My guess that risk of air attack exists first light today ... Well, air attack did not materialise this morning but at first light we left Stanley Harbour and proceeded round the coast a little way, to the entrance of Fitzroy settlement. Here, we patrolled a line 3 miles offshore and, after some considerable delay, commenced embarking Scots Guards who had been in the field. They came aboard from the helicopters with mud on their boots and carrying their heavy packs, which presumably contain everything they had needed.

Back at Port Stanley they moved into the inner anchorage, and more soldiers and baggage were transferred aboard.

> We now have on board the most people we have ever had and conditions below are really crowded. As well as every cabin being occupied, the upper car deck is now one vast barrack room with camp beds and kit crowding the whole deck from bow to stern. At mealtimes, the queues are enormous and stretch from the second-class cafeteria right through to the first-class area. All day today we have been re-provisioning by helicopter and by boat so that nearly all the time helicopters had been hovering with underslung loads or landing on our number one flight deck. Having meals has been compared to eating under the main runway at Heathrow.

Their particular task as an accommodation ship was taking shape, as they had nearly 1400 people on board, which posed particular problems in disposing of the garbage and providing food and water. The marked contrast between the activity while they were on passage and their new role caused difficulties in morale both for the crew and for the military personnel. In their role as an accommodation ship:

> We embarked General Menendez and company today, from *Fearless*. He was the head of the Argentine garrison here and surrendered to the British forces on 15 June. In order to accommodate General Menendez one engineer had to move cabin and Sandy the purser also. This was not very well received and there were rumblings in the mess room at dinnertime.

Towards the end of June most of the forces that they had carried had been disembarked, with exception of the Scots Guards, whom they were taking round to San Carlos. This happened on 29 June. On the last day of the month:

> Lying at San Carlos all day, we disembarked the last of the Scots Guards during the morning and they flew across the sound to Port Howard. At lunchtime we started to embark our 500 POWs. They were all searched and a lot of hidden

arms were found, including a complete rifle, plenty of ammunition and several pistols. Knives and bayonets were found in abundance. Later in the day we moved alongside *Anco Charger* and topped up with fuel and water. We sailed at 23.00 for Stanley and it was quite a pleasant experience, as the moon was giving quite a bit of light. Sailing with all our lights on made a change and we were accompanied by HMS *Ambuscade*. Fanning Head looked particularly impressive – silvery in the moonlight but no navigation lights – absolute isolation.

After their return to Port Stanley he complained that there would be nothing to write about if they carried on like that. Little did in fact happen, and the days continued quietly until, on 12 July:

At about 10.30 we heard from QHM [Queen's Harbour Master, the naval officer in command of the port] that our departure was imminent, and shortly afterwards [we were told] that we were off to Puerto Madryn at 18.00 tonight ... During the day, one of the guards accidentally fired his MG [machine gun] into the lift shaft. Bullet went straight through bulkhead, as though it had been drilled.

The next day, on passage at sea, he was much happier:

Great to be moving again, four engines, 17 knots – feels marvellous after hanging around so long. We are now making our way to Puerto Madryn, which we should reach tomorrow at about 08.00. One of our POWs speaks Welsh! This is obviously a relic from the Welsh settlement in Patagonia. In 1860, they settled around the Chubut area which includes Puerto Madryn ... How ironic, that this particular POW should be escorted to his homeland by a detachment of Welsh Guards. Towards the end of the watch there was a marvellous sight. The wind had freshened from the NNE and it was very dark. Then, at about 23.00, we passed into an area of pronounced bioluminescence. Each wave crest, each patch of foam, stood out against the pitch-black background with an eerie glow. Spray against bridge windows sparkled like momentary stars. Worth coming to see.

They arrived at Puerto Madryn the next morning to disembark their passengers:

We went alongside the Alumina jetty at Madryn at about 0800 and soon began to disembark our POWs. As General Menendez went ashore, a bugler sounded a mini-fanfare – quite well done. Then followed a succession of hugs and pats for the single Argie TV crew before the remainder of them went ashore. They certainly looked in good shape, one wore a red beret and carried his full pack including helmet, and gave a very jaunty salute. Then followed the conscripts and each was welcomed and directed to a coach to be taken off – where? I don't know but I would like to think it would eventually be home … We left and rang full away[6] at 11.00. We made 22 knots flat out. Our escort, an old ex-American destroyer, kept up but made lots of smoke.

They arrived back in San Carlos the next day to bunker from the *Anco Charger*, and to be met by a rumour that they were to embark civilian passengers to take them to the United Kingdom. Then they sailed back to Port Stanley to embark more Welsh Guards and civilian personnel. The next day the captain and SNO (senior naval officer) decided to sail at 10.30, although the QHM told them they were not due to sail until 12.30. Passing *Uganda*, now repainted in her normal colours, they proceeded to sea, their destination being changed shortly after so that they were now proceeding to Ascension Island. The passage there was without great incident, the diary entries becoming more and more brief until on 27 July they arrived at Ascension. As they arrived, a BP tanker was flying the Welsh flag in honour of the *St Edmund*'s passengers. When a message

---

[6] Signal on the bridge/engine-room telegraph that the ship was 'full away on passage' (FAOP) and that port manoeuvres were finished.

of thanks was sent across from the senior Welsh Guards officer, they replied, 'It is the least we can do – your front row is almost as good as Pontypool's'. It was decided by the SNO on board that Louis Roskell would be in charge of two ship's football teams, which would be taken ashore to have a game:

Told ... that I would be in charge of the party, my spirits sank somewhat when he told me of a long list of restrictions. Proceed directly to football pitch, not to remove shirts, not to visit cafés, bars, clubs, NAAFI, PX,[7] not to swim or behave in any way liable to be of any influence to the imported population of the island ... I enjoyed the heli-ride in a Sea King, then at the airport I mustered the 'teams' and was just giving them the dire warnings when in jumped the SNOAI [Senior Naval Officer Ascension Island] and asked 'who are you?' He then took over the show and once more, went through the ritual 'pre-flight briefing'. I was thoroughly choked off by this and went along with it for the sake of the others. We then managed a lift into Georgetown and were left by a level area of cinder known as a football pitch. The party then dispersed and I went in a Transit to the PX, a sort of forces general store where I browsed around for a while. Leaving the PX ... I was soon able to get a lift on the lorry ... This was the 'bus service' so I had a ride up to Two Boats and out to English Bay.

The view from Two Boats was classic, looking out and down from a great height towards a blue bay, with toy ships anchored in it. The contrast from the ship, and the past month or so, was complete. The breeze could be heard rustling through the palm and gum trees and flowers in red and mauve were superb. Whitewashed bungalows of the residents nestled into the hillside and all looked peaceful and pleasantly tropical. Toward English Bay the lunar aspect of the landscape was more

---

[7] Post Exchange, the American equivalent of the NAAFI.

pronounced and it was fantastic in the true sense, i.e. there was a dream-like quality about the hills and plains, like nothing I had seen before. Many hills of varying size had craters at the top. As to the colour it varied through cinder black and grey to a rich warm red. There were plains of apparently untouched pumice and, in the middle, large boulders thrown from the last explosion which occurred – when? It could have been last week, by the way the hills, barren of vegetation some of them, look just like heaps of cinders. In fact, geologically, the island is only about 700 years old.

On the next day, while receiving stores to take with them back to the Falklands, they watched the planes taking off for the UK without them. They sailed on the last day of July:

At 17.50 we started to heave in the anchor. We came round the bow of *Iris* and headed out to sea past *Alvega*, *British Esk* and *British Trent*. What a send-off! Sirens blared, flags dipped and we even fired our Very pistol in reply.

The passage back to the Falkland Islands was marred only by the news that they would be the accommodation ship in Port Stanley and the fact that they would probably not be relieved until mid-September at the earliest. Before they arrived there was some problem with the crew, and Louis Roskell was:

... told on watch of ... drunken assaults and threats in mess room 20 minutes before. This incident is a drink-related thing and there is the problem. On the way down, there were only three beers per man per day allowed and while everybody stuck to the rules this worked well and there was little trouble. Now, the rules relaxed, the boozers are back making trouble and causing misery for everyone else.

After a rough end to their trip, with gales causing them to reduce speed they arrived in San Carlos Water and bunkered from the *British Tay*, on which he commented that he saw his first female third mate. Back at Port Stanley, the next day they moved from their anchorage to pick up a mooring buoy. This is a standard operation for a ship:

> ... so what could be simpler? Everything went wrong. *Lively*, the harbour boat, took our mooring rope out to the buoy for us to heave up close. She made fast on the wrong side and ended up as a sandwich between our bow and the mooring buoy. When the big moment came to shackle us on, the shackle she had wouldn't fit. In the meantime, the ship, swinging gently in the breeze, started to crush *Lively* and at the same time our rope fouled the anchor. This was lifted gently and then deposited gently on *Lively*'s foredeck. She was horribly trapped and only got away with the greatest good fortune as we hove the mooring rope and simultaneously lifted the anchor for a moment. Thrusting to starboard washed *Lively* away from us and away she went to lick her wounds.

After this excitement days passed without much incident. On 27 August he was one of three, including the captain, who decided to check the lifeboats:

> ... to make sure they were working. A job that should have been done by our seamen. The deck crew seem to do their own thing. The ship on deck is a heap of rust and the gear is in a disgusting state. Some lifeboat limit switches could rust away soon.

With little to do as the days passed, the energies of some on board were diverted in other directions:

> Over the last week or so [some of the engineers] have been building a dummy funnel out of hardboard, and tonight was the night we were due to put it on the tin roof of the hulk which lies just in front of the cathedral ... After making careful plans during the day, zero hour was at 18.30. We donned our WRVS (*Women's Royal Volunteer Service, similar to the SAS*)[8] black boiler suits and moved quietly and efficiently down to the stern ramp where our

---

[8] Note that these are Louis Roskell's words, not an editorial comment!

lifeboat was waiting. At this time it was dark, but there were still enough boats around the harbour for us not to look conspicuous. Our lights were doused when near to the wreck and we went in. Brian and I climbed up onto the roof via a ladder which we had placed there early in the day whilst on a reconnaissance expedition. Brian passed a heaving line over the ridge which was made fast on the other side of the wreck then went up to the apex. Everything was very wet and slippery and he wouldn't have made it without the line. Once or twice boats came by and we had to lie flat and still so as not to be noticed, especially when one of the Kiwi launches passed its searchlight over the nearby anchored landing craft. Eventually, we hoisted the funnel up to the roof and placed it rather wonkily in position. We returned safely to the ship at 20.30 to celebrate.

The next morning he went ashore and, after morning service in the cathedral:

Coffee in vicarage and army officers pondered which idiots had placed the Sealink funnel on the wreck they could see out of the window. I agreed with them heartily about the idiot bit.

On Tuesday they had to go back to the wreck and re-erect the funnel, which had fallen down, again in the dark of the early evening. During the next morning the *Norland* arrived at Port Stanley:

No word about our changeover but during morning our reliefs came over and suddenly it's happened – it's over – at least as far as *St Edmund* is concerned. We showed them over the ship and after lunch we prepared to leave ... On board *Norland* I realised how heavy my luggage was and, I'm afraid, dropped the big suitcase down one flight of stairs.

The *Norland* sailed from Port Stanley at 17.00 on Friday 17 September for Ascension Island. The diary entries finished the next day, and the journal ends with a note describing their flight home by Hercules to RAF Lyneham, arriving back in UK at 18.00 on 28 September, being met by a coach to return them to Dovercourt.

Early in the journal, while they were on passage to Ascension Island, he had written:

> My thoughts now? I'm in limbo. I think wistfully of home but I'm not tearing to get back – I'll take it as it comes. I think it possible that I would be keen to get home if things were not such a disaster in the job, and I mean disaster. After all, what future is there? Sealink is committing suicide or rather the crews are.

After enjoying the leave he was due, Louis Roskell had a varied career – but 30 years later he is still involved in the marine industry and is an accomplished marine artist.

The master's tale

The captain who arrived to take over from Captain Stockman was Captain Don Jarvis. Apart from one return trip to Ascension Island, he was to spend the next six months in Port Stanley harbour.

The new crew met at Parkeston Quay, near Harwich, to be taken by coach to RAF Brize Norton, from where they flew to Ascension Island by RAF jet. Here they joined the *Norland*, to sail with a detachment of troops and their stores to the Falklands. They joined the *St Edmund* on 15 September, two weeks after setting out from Harwich. The original crew (including Louis Roskell), whom they had relieved, returned on the *Norland* to go home on leave.

It was a very different environment to what they were used to. Don Jarvis noted in his diary that it was 'another cold and windy day. Tried all day to get better acclimatised ... Very rough weather.' A few days later he commented again, among the day's events: 'Went ashore ... Went to the hospital then on to NAAFI etc. Back on 11 a.m. boat with the general. Terrible gales all day. Lifeboat damaged. Blew like a bastard. Not feeling well.'

The days settled into a regular pattern. The *St Edmund* remained on her mooring in Port Stanley harbour for the remainder of September and all of October, carrying out her role as a floating hotel for more than a hundred troops and a detachment of Gurkhas. Clearly, time was hanging heavily for, on Wednesday 29 September he records that he 'cleaned officers' bathroom and engineers' wash place. After lunch pottered.' Cleaning bathrooms was not a normal activity for the captain! Nor was this, a few days later: ' ... spent afternoon cleaning carpet.'

The weather was a constant source of comment and interest in his diary. On 8 October, 'woke up to a gale and snow', and the next day, 'this morning the capital is covered in a thick blanket of snow – unbelievable. A gale blew all day.'

On Remembrance Sunday, 14 November, he represented the Merchant Navy at the service in Port Stanley Cathedral. On the same day the *Norland* broke down and was unable to sail to Ascension Island. The regiment that was returning aboard her transferred to the *St Edmund*. They sailed the next day, and he commented 'weather better, but can't trust it.' However, the weather held and he recorded that the ship was doing 18 knots. They arrived at Ascension, took bunkers from the tanker *Alvega* and then anchored to disembark the troops who were going home and receive the Hampshire Regiment, who had arrived to go south. Two days later they sailed, and arrived on 4 December, entering San Carlos Water in thick fog to refuel from the *British Trent*. They then moved to Fox Bay for the Chinooks to take the troops ashore in an operation which continued for the rest of that day and all the following day.

Arriving back at Port Stanley on 6 December, they settled back into their role as a hotel ship. An ongoing problem for Captain Jarvis was the attitude of the crew. Although they had volunteered, they had been planning to go on strike the previous spring, before the ship was taken up from trade. As a result there was trouble from the outset. Before they had boarded the plane, they had expected the Captain to pay for all their food. After boarding the *Norland* in Ascension they demanded the same standard of cabins as the officers and to be able to use the officers' bar. On being refused, the leader of the deputation refused to sail on the ship. When asked to disembark, he refused to leave. In the Falklands, the Sealink sign along the side of the ship had to be painted out to reduce the visibility of the ship. The crew refused to do the job, so Don Jarvis and the chief officer had to do it. Because of where they were, the crew could not be sacked, so the troubles continued.

Despite the atmosphere on board, a children's party was held on the *St Edmund*, complete with a band and Father Christmas. The Christmas season was marked by several parties, including a curry lunch hosted on board and many other parties ashore.

Don Jarvis's diary for 1983 opens with 'Spent the early hours of today dancing at the Governor's House – a very good evening it was too ... slept at Governor's House, back on board in afternoon.' The excitement of the New Year had dissipated a few days later, when he noted that he was 'bored to tears'. The boredom was banished a few days later, however, when he noted, 'Great excitement – Margaret Thatcher arriving ... Onto the airport road for the arrival.' The excitement grew when, on 11 January, he met Admiral Fieldhouse, the Commander-in-Chief Fleet, in the morning and, 'in the evening went to the Governor's House – marvellous, marvellous, marvellous, M Thatcher and co. – superb'. His enthusiasm was undimmed the next day, when he described himself as 'a devoted servant of the Tories after that speech. Absolutely wonderful.'

Before Christmas a floating hotel block had arrived and had moved to a permanent site alongside the quay. The role of the *St Edmund* was winding down, and three days later the *Cunard Countess* arrived with, among others, a relief crew for the *St Edmund*. The ratings all signed off, to go home, the officers staying to take the ship home. He then received 'the news that the ship is going home for refit and to be sold,' which 'came as quite a shock ... Hope we can get away by 7 February – but how quickly orders can change in this place.' They 'signed off the 46 people without too much hassle ... even P. and H. [two of the major troublemakers] went quietly!! After lunch, to get away from all the hassle decided to go on a fishing trip. Most successful, caught three fish.'

The new crew signed on the next day. He celebrated the

departure of the old crew the day after the *Cunard Countess* sailed, having 'a marvellous evening with the 37th Engineer Regiment. Back on board for 1.15 a.m. – feeling rather tired to say the least.'

By this time there was much insecurity over the future, with the news that Sealink were withdrawing from the Harwich to Hook of Holland route, following the collapse of negotiations with the National Union of Seamen. The crew organised a ballot on the ship to decide their view on the future of the Hook of Holland service: '29 for, 20 against and 10 abstentions. Stupid buggers really.'

Despite this comment, the new crew were more amenable than those who had left, and he notes that 'the lads were able to do a bit more painting of the ship's side.' His social life continued apace: 'In the evening attended a cocktail party, then back for meal with 37 REs.'

The orders to depart were confirmed for 8 February, so they weighed anchor at 10.00 and 'left the harbour amidst a marvellous farewell – all ships whistled etc.' As they started the return trip the weather was not good; after being in port for a long time it must have come as an unpleasant shock. 'Ship pitching, rolling and pounding to near-gale northerly winds ... ship most uncomfortable.' Despite the weather, the crew were busy cleaning the ship after her long stay in port: 'Crew cleaning car decks. Stewards washing out cabins on B and C decks. Everywhere is littered with army filth.'

The bad weather returned in earnest: 'tremendous gales over night and all day today. Force 10 and 11 northerly – and the rain!! Absolutely torrential for 24 hours; ship flooded in places ... Ship behaved very well if uncomfortable. Got no sleep at all due to the banging about and all the gear moving around'. However, the weather did abate, and after eight days they arrived at Ascension Island where they refuelled alongside the tanker *Alvega*, before sailing on the next leg of the trip, to Las Palmas. Taking on more bunker fuel there, they sailed, after a six-hour stop, for Portsmouth, where they were to offload the extra lifeboats they had been carrying. Four days later they anchored off Portsmouth and the lifeboats were taken off, but their departure for their final destination of Wallsend was delayed for a day by dense fog. Captain Jarvis's diary also ends abruptly, on 28 February 1983: 'Arrive Wallsend.'

All the Sealink crew left the *St Edmund* and a new chapter in her life began, under the ownership of the Ministry of Defence and a new name, the *Keren*. She was to continue serving the Falkland Islands under that name, but with a different crew, for some while longer.

6

The repair ships and tugs

Stena Inspector

Yorkshireman

Irishman

Salvageman

Stena Inspector

The two sister ships *Stena Inspector* and *Stena Seaspread* were highly technical vessels, designed for both diving and surface support, primarily for the offshore oil industry. Their special features included a stabilising system which reduced the ships' rolling by up to three-quarters, cranes of up to 100 tonnes lift, workshop and storage areas and a dynamic positioning system. This system of high-precision position fixing, coupled with the ships' five propellers, enabled them to keep to a position within 3 metres in gale-force winds.

They had accommodation for over 100, but their standard Merchant Navy crew was just 29. Despite the availability of spare berths, more had to be provided for the personnel of the naval party that joined, which exceeded 150 in number.

The *Stena Seaspread* was involved from the start, repairing eleven battle-damaged warships, including *Arrow*, *Plymouth*, *Glamorgan* and *Broadsword*. In addition she carried out other repairs and maintenance to Royal Fleet Auxiliary and merchant ships.

In late May, it became apparent to the Ministry of Defence that further repair facilities would be needed, and so the *Stena Inspector* was chartered on 25 May. At that time she was under the Swedish flag, so she had to be re-registered and the Swedish crew replaced by British Merchant Navy officers and crew.

On the same day, Captain David Ede, together with the chief engineer, the chief steward and the electrician flew to Savannah, in Georgia, USA, where the ship was in dry dock. They joined the ship on 26 May.

The captain's diary

Quite apart from the official logs that had to be kept, like others who were involved in Operation Corporate, David Ede kept a personal diary, which started on the day of his arrival in Savannah and ended on the day that he left the ship in October to fly home on leave. On Wednesday 26 May he noted:

Boarded *Stena Inspector*... Considerable dry-dock work to

complete. Received word that registry change complete at 11.45 BST. British flag raised at 14.00. Considerable bother from press and TV stations. British officers looking after re-classification with Dick Burrows of DoT ... Swedes attending to dry-dock work.

The problems with the press continued, and two days later he noted:

Ludicrous press statements appearing. Still inundated with reporters. Commander Barry Austin got in touch with embassy in Washington. They requested I talk to reporters and on TV in news broadcast to give simple statement of facts and stop speculation. Did so, denying knowledge of any orders etc. and being very specific about non-Swedish involvement.

It was clear, however, that although the ship was now re-registered the Swedes were still involved, for he noted on Saturday 29 May:

All work continues, rather chaotic but getting done – some problem with Swedish attitudes at lower levels but best ignored. RF getting a bit uptight don't blame him. With classification and all the ER [engine room], he's got a job on. Now Swedes asking for inventory. Told Swedes they must handle it themselves. Should have been done long ago and Brits got enough on their plates.

On Monday 31 May they were able to leave the dry dock:

Flooded up and left the dock just after 04.00 and proceeded downriver about 40 miles out to sea. Still shallow but can just do DP [dynamic positioning] trials. All trials ... went well. One or two hiccups, not a lot. All pretty good by 20.00. Headed for Charleston. Intend to get there early and get a few hours sleep in.

Berthed 0100 [1 June]. Captain Peter Strickland RN boarded to meet me. Seems okay ... Now in Charleston Navy Yard. Warships all over the place. RN, MoD and US Navy guys descended en masse at 08.00. Work started humming. Lot to do in five days. Everybody anxious to please everyone else. All realise important to make a success of this. 10 month charter, with 12 month option (or option to buy). Good rates for Stena – they must be laughing ... Press and TV started again but in Navy Yard no way they can get at us, thank goodness.

By the end of that week, on Friday 4 June:

All NP [naval party] 2010 moved aboard today and commenced storing ship. What a pile of work that is. Getting on well with the fixtures and fittings ... Getting to be a hell of a pile on deck. Sat com and satnav in and working. I'm glad we've got the latter – would be difficult without it down south. Invited with JW to HR (USN liaison) for dinner ... Food not special but pleasant evening.

The delivery of stores continued the next day, so he felt he had to help:

Stores situation hotting up. Put boiler suit on and went down to help with humping. Very nearly killed me after two hours but at least showed willing. Got all the personal gear I need now. Had three khaki uniforms delivered, pretty good, look smart. All officers fitted out with them. We went to PX [Post Exchange] today and bought stereos, TV games, tapes etc. for the ship. Spent about $2000, JW didn't mind and much appreciated by the ship. RN personnel all a bit stunned by general excellence of conditions and generosity – a good start.

The next day, Sunday 6 June, was not a day of rest:

A day of chaotic hard work. Aim was to sail by 12.00 ... JW and C/O both unhappy with stowage of stores. Went to inspect myself – recipe for disaster. Tons of flat plate steel just placed on deck and surrounded by hundreds of gas bottles. The Argentinians needn't bother – we were going to blow ourselves up. Told Captain Strickland no way we were going to sail in those conditions. Realised for the first time all RN (except X/O) [executive officer] are engineers, they haven't a clue about seamanship. I turned all my officers to, we split into groups ... ran ops., and RN doing what they were told, gradually re-stowed, tommed off, chocked etc. until I was reasonably satisfied that with due regard to good forecast it was safe to sail. ... Sailed 18.00 and proceeded to sea.

Their progress, however, was not without initial problems:

Good weather, work in progress sorting and re-stowing stores. Heading direct for Ascension Island. All seemed smooth until 19.30 when informed that doctor diagnosed cook with perforated ulcer. USCG [United States Coast Guard] contacted, chopper rendezvous arranged and diverted ship back towards Cape Canaveral. We lose 20 hours over this – what a way to go to war ... Chopper landed at 05.00 to take cook to Patrick Air Force Base. Doctor reckons he would die within 24 hours without surgery. Lucky we weren't another 24 hours out at sea. Back on course. Getting little worried about RN working hours. Seems they [are] only doing 08.00–16.00. Will leave for a day or two to see if just taking a breather after Charleston.

By the Thursday 10 June it had become apparent that:

RN definitely working less than eight-hour day, also appears going to do half day Saturday and Sunday off. Protested officially to Capt Strickland that if this was to be pattern I must insist that the steel and other dangerous cargo was racked safely first and his other work done later. He agreed. All hands to start tomorrow and priority job to make racks and clear steel from main deck and vertrep [vertical replenishment, i.e. helicopter landing] deck. Attack under way. *Sir Galahad* and *Sir Tristram* wiped out. *Plymouth* hit – paying a heavy price down there.

Another of the crew had become unwell:

He seems very unhappy – heard from several sources. Sent for him. He says he wasn't told we were going to danger zone – doesn't want to. Also has blood pressure problem and short of stabilising pills. Doctor doesn't have any. No choice but to send him home from Ascension Island [on] both psychological and medical grounds. No harm done, will give RN another cabin if they give me a man as substitute AB. They agreed to this. Steel stowage going well now. Have given up hope of having ship painted up by Ascension Island. Glad if all is secured and stowed and ship clear.

The stowage was completed next day and he was satisfied about the ship's safety if they were to hit bad weather. As a result, on Sunday 13 June:

Gave our men the day off today. They've earned a break and the RN not overworking. Read the lesson at the church service – only MN rep there.

The next day:

The Argentinians have surrendered. Does this mean all conflict ended or only on Falkland Islands? If the former the war bonus ends (before we've even started). Don't think any of us intend a long tour if there is no bonus. Why should we, it's then just another contract.

Their passage to Ascension Island continued, and they arrived on 21 June:

Arrived A.I. at 06.00. All is chaos. Not very many ships here now. Waiting for stores to come out by lighter for many hours. Mail came aboard but nothing for me. Felt pretty rotten about it ... Rest of NP2010 boarded, now 160 RN personnel. Have also had confirmed that Admiral D Reffell and his staff of 33 boarding tomorrow for us to transport to rendezvous with *Invincible* and *Bristol* ... Most things on board okay. Looks like we've got problems with the diving system – or at least with the divers' ability to operate it. Still, should have time to sort it out. Lighters eventually arrived starting 16.30 – got three before dark, two more tomorrow. Ship in blacked-out condition, still chance of

Argentinian submarines, apparently. Ascension Island is pretty barren and bleak, no attraction to go ashore. What a lot through the past weeks. Apparently at the height (about 24 April) there were 500 aircraft movements in the day – making it the busiest airfield in the world.

The next day the admiral boarded with his staff:

Admiral Reffell aboard by helo at 12.00, followed by his staff in batches. All accommodated, have got a young commander sharing my cabin. Very bright young man – I'm told in fifteen years he'll be the First Sea Lord, I shouldn't be surprised. Met the admiral and welcomed him aboard. He is an extremely distinguished looking man with a shy and totally courteous manner. Found myself instinctively calling him 'sir'. Had to go alongside *Alvega* for bunkers – he came on bridge to watch manoeuvres. All went well and he was most impressed with handling capabilities of ship. ... Able to sail spot on 17.00 as stated.

The day after they sailed he described as a quiet, beautiful day. However, on the next day, the Thursday:

Problems with satellite communications and they have no manufacturer's handbook. Answer: get in touch with C-in-C Fleet and arrange for Nimrod to drop one to us by parachute – great what you can arrange when money no object. Nimrod appeared about 11.30 so stopped ship and launched Zodiac. Nimrod then made two runs and dropped the manual and some mail – including yesterday's newspapers – incredible.

The next day was equally eventful:

What a day – fantastic. If I have to leave the sea and take a shore job I'm going out on a high note. We had some hours in hand for the rendezvous. A chopper came out at 10.30 to take Admiral Reffell to *Invincible*. We proceeded to R/V where only *Iris* waited. Then as time passed, up came *Bristol*, then *Invincible*, then *Ambuscade*, and finally *British Tay*. At 13.30 we were ordered to positions and by

14.00 we were in convoy. At that time the whole operation began. We were steaming at 12 knots with helicopters everywhere, it was terrific – I'm glad I was part of it. Who'd have ever thought I'd be in command of the most sophisticated merchant vessel in formation with an RN flotilla at close quarters.

At 14.30 received instructions from *Bristol* to strike the admiral's flag as all his staff were now transferred ... I went up on the heli-deck to take some photographs and someone pointed out the pilot of the Sea King that was doing part of the transfer. Sure enough it was Prince Andrew, laughing and waving to us all. The only other thing I would like to have seen was the Harrier on the deck of *Invincible* just ahead take off – but that didn't happen. The operation went on to 18.00 when our last lift was taken and we received orders from *Invincible* to peel off and proceed as ordered. We did and proceeded in calm conditions to St Helena.

They arrived there on Monday 28 June and he was able to go ashore:

Arrived St Helena at 08.30. Thought it looked very Madeira like and continued to think so. Temperature ranges same and when I saw the type of scenery and roads ... became certain of it. Went ashore at 09.30. Met the governor and he invited us to lunch on our return if timing right. Then driven on very quick (2 hour) tour of island. Scenery, mountains, valleys, etc. grand and very volcanic but good soil. Up to Napoleon's house, faithfully preserved, very interesting but not enough time to appreciate it all ... Islanders all very friendly, but everything too much of a Victorian backwater to produce much enlightenment. Went on to governor's house (Plantation House) and met Jonathan the ancient tortoise. Huge old fellow reputed to have been there in Napoleon's time. Loved having his photo taken and his neck stroked ... Got back to ship 12.30, sailed for Ascension Island at 13.30 with 30 locals on board for delivery. Supposed to be bringing 30 back but this could change. Rough cost of this ferry work £250,000 – stupid.

On the next day, at sea:

Had a damage control exercise. I'm not particularly impressed. I do not approve of RN way of running to stations. To my mind it is dangerous to the individual and likely to create panic. Never mind, that's their business. Talked with X/O about the speed of work of his men. He says he'll improve things. St Helenians willingly helped on the big stores shift. Did a good job, saved us a lot of time – they've been absolutely no trouble.

They arrived at Ascension Island on the last day of June:

Approaching A. I. at 1130 when Chinook appeared from nowhere and wanted to land the sat com man. He came down okay so the heli-deck can take this size chopper. Arrived with mail also. We arrived at A.I. at 13.30 and despite the usual chaotic delays with stores we got all wanted ... sailed at 19.00 with 22 passengers for St Helena. Aim is to arrive first light Saturday, stay all day and, if possible, until daylight Sunday.

July did not start on a good note:

Worst weather experienced so far. Heading right into gale. Hitting some pretty hard, slowed down to approx. 10 knots. At this rate will be lucky to make it for daylight on Saturday. Main deck awash. I think RN slowly learning what they will face down south. Poor Islanders, mainly seasick. Everybody on a downer – me especially ... Can't do anything and it's affecting my work. Getting unfairly short-tempered with men and really they are doing well. At present can't see being relieved until October at earliest.

As he had hoped, they arrived at St Helena on the Saturday morning:

Arrived St Helena 09.30. During night, change of orders,

now going South Georgia. What one might call a varied day. Swung the compass on arrival and seemed to have done a remarkable job – deviations reduced by 90 per cent.

He received an invitation, with some others from the ship, to lunch at Plantation House, the governor's residence:

Left ship about 12, met by car taken to Government House ... Pleasant place, high up so quite chilly. Big open fire in drawing room was lovely. Drinks then lunch (very ordinary) but good conversation. After lunch ... Four of us stayed in the lounge talking the afternoon away, very relaxing and pleasant. ... Obviously H.E. of St Helena a pretty lonely post with little support from London ... Decided to leave about 18.00, have a couple of beers in town with the 'lads' and get back early. Went fine until we left to walk to jetty – caught in rain and at jetty found boats had been cancelled until 22.30. Walk back, getting wetter, arrange to get boats back on ... finished up eating fish and chips in damp conditions.. From governor's house lunch to fish and chips in eight hours – sublime to ridiculous. Back aboard 20.30. The [crew] started arriving back at 23.00, all aboard by midnight – usual cuts, broken noses etc., etc., but there had been plenty of booze and plenty of girls apparently so they had had a good run. Good luck to them – there won't be any runs ashore for a long time now. It was worth a visit, but I don't think I'd like to stay there very long after all.

All the crew had returned by shortly after midnight, so they weighed anchor and sailed about 00.30. He noted in his diary:

Ordinary day at sea, good speed made – still haven't found my 'tropical' weather. It will be getting cold soon. Looks like we're going to South Georgia to build a garrison quarters, work on the Argentinian submarine and possibly repairs on HMS *Brilliant*. Well, it's a change isn't it?

The next day, 5 July, they had received instructions for the work they were to do in South Georgia:

> Good progress this day. Received instructions on what we will do in S.G. Includes salvage of Argentine submarine *Santa Fe* (beach it if safe, tow away and sink it if not), repair of Grytviken jetty, building barracks, repairing boats and vehicles, helping *Wimpey Seahorse* lay mooring buoys with our divers. Quite a programme. Could be there for some while. Still not getting anywhere with either diet or stopping cigarettes – seem to have no willpower any more. What on earth happened to the drive and determination I once had? Painting on ship coming along – nearly all done by MN lads. These RN fellows are really of little use to us.

In his next day's entry he commented further on the works facing them in South Georgia:

> Quite a varied routine in the most appalling conditions. Apparently almost continuous blizzards and even the penguins have disappeared. Stopped the ship for half an hour and completed painting the transom. Did a thorough inspection of the ship and particularly well deck. Must say things are now well stowed and about as secure as can be done. Still feel will suffer a certain amount of damage and loss when we hit the heavy seas but it shouldn't be extensive. Maybe problems with freezing conditions re lube oil ... will have to watch that carefully.

As they progressed towards South Georgia he noted that the weather was deteriorating, and he anticipated an unpleasant few days ahead. In addition:

> The ship's characters are beginning to establish themselves, and the anonymous newsletter is very good. I must start keeping them. 'No-Neck' [one of the divers] fined £140 for drunkenness and other related charges. Stiff fines in the RN.

The anticipated bad weather materialised on the next day:

> First taste of bad weather. Between 09.00 and 09.30 the wind and sea went from light northwesterly to force 10

southerly. Down to 5½ knots and one or two awkward stops due problems with main propeller. Didn't last too long however, about 12 hours, then we slowly increased to full speed again ... We hope about four days maximum [in South Georgia], so can reach F.I. and have a day with *Seaspread* before she sails.

On the following day, Saturday 10 July, they had the opportunity to send mail home:

Weather had died right away during the night. At about 10.30 the *Nordic Ferry* hove into sight on her way to A.I. and the UK. We decided to do a mail transfer. She picked a course and steamed at 6 knots, I hove close alongside and a line was fired across and our mail bag transferred, all went smoothly. Captain Jennings said icebergs started about 150 miles south. Good weather continued throughout the day and right on cue, the first bergs appeared at about 22.30. Doubled the watches with Turnbull/Mound on nights, Vail/Ramsden on days. John Turnbull has had five years in command and plenty of ice experience on Manchester Liners so is a good hand to have.

The icebergs continued the next day:

Plenty of impressive icebergs this morning ... Did a bit of weaving in and out. 1½ miles off the biggest ... Bridge absolutely crowded with RN onlookers. I don't mind but it is getting pretty full and a little too much clutter for the watch keepers. I might have to put a block on it soon.

At the beginning of the next week they arrived at South Georgia:

Managed to arrive anchorage Grytviken at 15.15, 17 hours ahead of schedule – I'd never have believed it. Only one really serious blow the whole voyage. The approach to South Georgia very dramatic. The island almost totally white with stark peaks and crags and enormous glaciers running smoothly into the sea. Inevitably there was an iceberg in the middle of the entrance to Cumberland Bay but it was easily avoided and the final run to Grytviken was down the rather awe-inspiring fjord. Arrival very anticlimactic. Smallest village in England is bigger, but nice to see the other ships (*Endurance, Yorkshireman*, etc). *Yorkshireman* came alongside to take some RN personnel over to *Endurance*. Maybe they will bring back some mail. No such luck. They returned with nothing but information. Off tomorrow to do the diving job in Stromness.

The diving job in Stromness brought with it some difficulties:

Working parties landed and went to Stromness arriving 11.30 ... Some bad feeling with diving bosun because I question his intention to dive in these waters to 180 feet on air in ordinary suits. Resolved in the end by him saying he was limiting water time to 20 minutes (instead of original 50 which he agreed was madness). I pretended I had misunderstood about 50 minutes – I hadn't! ! And it blew over but he's feeling very anti – too bad ... Saw the dive started and picked up by Wasp to fly to Leith. Very open and cold but exhilarating ... Went rambling round Leith. Amazing amount of equipment and stores lying there – buildings vandalised, a great pity. Marvellous feeling, thigh-deep in snow but with the proper gear could stumble round warm and dry – thoroughly enjoyed it. Returned about 16.30 by chopper, diving ops finished successfully, got rest of shore party back, sailed for Grytviken.

The work continued the next day:

Sailed for Stromness 09.00. On DP 50 m from the beach at 10.30 and work parties landed to gather timber for Grytviken jetty repair. *Wimpey Seahorse* arrived 11.30 to grapple for mooring chain – if she gets it divers will go in. *Yorkshireman* arrived 13.00 to load the timber aboard. No luck with grapple and work abandoned at 16.00. Two king penguins appeared on the beach, what a lovely sight, they were like little old men ... Grytviken at 18.30 and anchored for night. Looks as if submarine is afloat. They'll probably beach her tomorrow. We won't see it as we must return to Stromness – pity.

As a result of the official ceasefire, which was agreed on 12 July, the 150 per cent war bonus paid to the Merchant Navy crews ceased to be operative. This caused some dissatisfaction on board, and both the National Union of Seamen and the Merchant Navy Officers Association had become involved, as had the ship's owners. Messages had gone from the ship to both unions and negotiations were ongoing as to the level of bonus which was to be paid from that date and the pay arrangements. This was an issue that was to continue for some time without being resolved to the crew's entire satisfaction. However, the work continued, interspersed with some light relief:

Grytviken party off at 05.30, sailed to Leith and put ashore smaller work party who will stay two or three days. Then into Stromness. Weather not so good, [*Wimpey*] *Seahorse* couldn't work until 12.00. Our divers didn't get in until 15.10 then had a problem with diver who had to be recompressed. I don't agree with air diving to this depth in these icy waters. Anyway, nothing achieved today in the way of diving. Another work party ashore in Stromness fixing up the place a bit ... Sailed for Grytviken at 16.30. Anchored for the night. Submarine successfully floated and beached. Invited to *Endurance* by Nick Barker [commanding officer] ... for dinner. Very pleasant evening, Barker a very pleasant man with some very funny stories. He has a great fondness, really love, of the Antarctic and full of plans to work down here after leaving RN. Says there is great deal of oil and gold, uranium, etc. (Lovely story of young RN lad in VD queue responding to doctor saying 'I don't know what I'll tell your father', 'Nor do I, sir, but you'd better make up your mind bleeding fast, he's next in!') All boats frozen up, had to return by Zodiac [fast rigid inflatable boat], but even that, though cold, had an eerie beauty.

The hard work continued on the Friday:

> Off to Stromness again. Lot of growlers about but a beautiful day. No problems this time and jobs (divers) completed at last, unless *Wimpey Seahorse* comes up with another problem. The lads left ashore in Leith seemed happy (even got streetlights working) but I bet they'll be glad to be picked up by Sunday. Returned to Grytviken by 16.30. *Endurance*, *Salvageman* and *Yorkshireman* gone. *Stena Inspector* now I/C South Georgia (and post box) with only *Wimpey Seahorse* and Army here.

After a busy week, he gave the crew a day off and, the next day, Sunday, he:

> ... went off ashore to Grytviken. Wading through the snow to the church, which is not vandalised and in a remarkable state of preservation. Everything else is more or less a shambles. Who would ramble around thigh-deep in snow in a ruined village – we must be mad. Still, I enjoyed it – it was rather invigorating. Found a harpoon head, fragmentation type – might make a nice table lamp if I can get it home. Went round to Leith to revictual the shore party. They all seem as happy as Larry and want to stay to Tuesday.

On Tuesday they duly returned to Leith to collect the shore party:

> Went off to Leith to get them aboard. Performed a rather tricky piece of ship handling to take on some welding sets and compressors from jetty. Quite pleased with myself. Crane over stern and holding her like so. [A small hand-drawn diagram at the foot of the page shows the ship's stern onto the jetty, with kelp to one side, buoys to either side of the bow and a 30 knot wind blowing onto the port side of the ship.]

The following day he had the opportunity to see another of the local landmarks:

Went ashore at King Edward Point today and visited the army at Shackleton House, invited them on board for lunch and a look around. Got some snowshoes and walked up to Shackleton Monument. Super views ... came back about noon with the army officers, pleasant couple of hours. Mail due to arrive on *Leeds Castle* now tomorrow at 08.00. About 17.00 wind started gusting up, reached 56 knots and about three hours of very strong winds. Ship held on DP perfectly, instant reaction from thruster with increase of wind speed, never moved more than a couple of metres ... a very impressive performance by the DP in my opinion.

The *Leeds Castle* arrived with mail and stores so they were able to sail for a rendezvous with RFA *Regent*, into a heavy sea, for a stores transfer. The rendezvous finally happened two days later:

Made new rendezvous at 10.00 but after delays vertrep [helicopter transfer] called off due rough weather. Told to hang about and try again later. Job finally done at 16.00. Eight hours for the sake of 30 minutes' work. Proceeded on slow speed for Stanley.

They arrived in Port Stanley the next day:

Anchored in Port William. Lots of choppers buzzing about and decisions being made. No snow anywhere, scenery very like Shetland, except for masses of ships about. Mostly MN but some RN minesweepers and the destroyer *Avenger* – our first real job. Invited aboard for lunch with Captain Hugo White. *Avenger* has been down from start. Shot down one Exocet with 4.5 inch gun and missed another by just 5 feet ... Got back 14.30. The big fenders we'd needed arrived so fixed on and proceeded to *Avenger*. Alongside and tied up, she upped her anchor I moved us where we wanted to be and dropped two anchors. All went very well ... I'm looking forward to a good look round her (Type 21). Should be alongside for at least two days. Mainly repairing bad cracks in her aluminium superstructure.

On Wednesday 28 July he records that it was a

> ... very blustery day. Winds up to 66 knots. *Cedarbank* and *Tor Caledonia* dragged and grounded. Went aboard *Avenger* and showed round the operations and fighting centre. Quite something, though a lot of it above my head of course. Captain down there, not on bridge when in battle, must seem very odd ... Seem to be getting some niggles from junior RN officers. Can't help it much. Why do juniors always seem more conscious of position than senior officers? Letters from *Seaspread* indicate similar there ... Anchor holding amazingly well, but a terrific strain, two ships on just one anchor wire.

The work on the *Avenger* was completed the next day and she sailed at 10.00, being replaced by the *Birmingham* half an hour later. There was pressure to accommodate more ships:

> QHM [Queen's Harbour Master] keeps pressing to have two ships (the second, in this case, *Apollo*) alongside. Still refusing until I get the Artemis working.[1] They've got it as far as the chopper base but what a job to get it fixed up. The site has to be cleared of mines for a start. Spent a couple of hours clearing crossed anchor wires – at least we can do it easily on here. Must say anchor position being held better than I expected.

One of the repairs to the *Birmingham* was the replacement of the radar pedestal and aerial. Captain Roger Villar noted in his book that:

> Some very specialised work was done including replacing the main radar aerial in the destroyer HMS *Birmingham* in a 35 knot wind. The Dockyard at home had said this could only be done by them in calm conditions. That it was possible at all is due in great part to the extraordinary skill

---

[1] Artemis was a device to assist with accurate position keeping for the dynamic positioning system.

of the Merchant Navy crane driver.[2]

David Ede's diary entry for this notes:

> Completed the replacement of radar pedestal on *Birmingham* – Portsmouth said it couldn't be done. Tony Burnett (crane driver) did highly skilled and excellent job.

On the next day he managed to talk his way

> ... into a helicopter ride in *Apollo*'s Lynx. Sat with legs dangling outside zooming all over the harbour. Cold and a little frightening ... Also went over to Port Stanley Airport. Lots of broken planes on the ground. Plenty of activity, but what a godforsaken place. Some of the lads went ashore and got postcards but that is the most exciting thing. Got the Artemis working at last, which gives a bit of bad weather assurance.

It appears that weather conditions had been such that *Birmingham* had not been able to remain alongside, as he notes:

> Artemis working well, went into DP anchor assist and allowed *Birmingham* back alongside starboard. *Apollo* and *Yorkshireman* to port so quite a gaggle of ships on us. Sat very well throughout the day even with winds to 46 knots.

On Monday 2 August he noted that it was a slow day, with little of note on which to comment. Although the *Birmingham* had sailed, the *Apollo* was still alongside. There was a slight diversion:

> *Apollo* sailor fined £30 for peeing in our alleyway – I thought 5p was steep!

Three days later another RN sailor caused him some amusement:

> Lovely incident of a J/R [junior rating] leading one of his oppos [friends] into my cabin at 23.00 – 'just showing him round, sir'– I rolled up laughing.

---

[2] R Villar, *Merchant Ships at War*. London, 1984, 73.

The young man in question apologised to him the next morning. (Subsequently, Captain Ede added to this story: he was entertaining five RN captains in his cabin at the time; the rating was unabashed by the presence of the captains, pointing out his own captain [Captain Strickland], his oppo's captain and Captain Ede. The next morning, the latter advised the young man to apologise to Captain Strickland quickly, before he was found and reprimanded!)

At the end of that week, on Saturday:

> *Bacchante* sailed 08.00, Tony Lyddon [the commanding officer] wearing his Stena Offshore cap. *Avenger* berthed starboard side, then *Birmingham* port side ... Plus *Falkland Sound* and *Tiger Bay* outside the warships – all resting on our DP system. Thank goodness the storm has passed and today is totally calm.

Clearly the totally calm weather did not continue into that night, and he was not impressed by Royal Naval seamanship:

> Warned *Birmingham* last night she had too few ropes out. She ignored advice. During the night she broke away and damaged our gangway. Called C/O and told him what I thought of his OOW [officer of the watch].

The start of the next week saw them sailing out of Port Stanley to Port San Carlos to set up another Artemis. On Tuesday 10 August:

> By first light it was a really lovely morning, clear and virtually flat calm. No need to go all the way to Port San Carlos for chopper rendezvous. Met outside and saved some steaming. Artemis taken by Chinook to Pebble Island and set up ... Picked it up quickly. *Brecon* had taken a transponder and dropped it near the wreck ... Got good readings of everything so *Seaspread* should find it easily.

The delayed rendezvous with *Scottish Eagle*, to take bunkers, eventually took place on Thursday that week:

> First line to *Scottish Eagle* at 08.30. Dense fog, very calm. Sailed round to PWS [Prince William Sound] in dense fog –

a bit hairy weaving through the anchored ships. Declined to have anyone alongside since I considered the anchorage (proper one occupied by *Saxonia*) unsafe and did not have the Artemis working.

By the next day they had clearly moved to a safer anchorage. There was further trouble with a Royal Navy ship:

Diomede berthed at 0830 alongside. Got Artemis going and berthed *Danae* at 10.30. *Diomede* got roasting from PS [senior naval officer on *Inspector*] and me on bridge. When told he couldn't come alongside at 0100 signalled Admiral Reffell, who sent snotty signal to PS, as a result of which men dragged out [of bunks] at 05.00. I showed [her commanding officer] why we had declined her earlier arrival; he said he 'hadn't understood' situation. I said in future ask us before firing off signals to admiral. Then PS jumped on him for discourtesy and told him there were two captains on this ship to ask. He went off with tail between legs. (He also handled his ship badly). Got rid of *Diomede* at 17.00.

At the end of the week gales had set in, up to force 9 inside the harbour and hurricane force 12 outside. He noted on Sunday 22 August:

Pretty wild and blustery day, no movements of small boats. *Cedarbank* dragged [her anchor], *Yorkshireman* tried to help her but she drifted still. Decided to go out to sea and went full ahead, severely damaged *Yorkshireman* (lots of splits, sixteen, in sides). She made it out, then couldn't get head to wind. Drifted along coast going full astern before she eventually got round. Nasty. *Avenger's* cracks opened up again so she came in at 20.00 for emergency repairs as she is due to sail home tomorrow.

Talk of some of the crew being relieved was confirmed when news came that the first wave of reliefs was due to arrive about 17 September. He, too, was keen to be relieved and hoped to leave about two weeks after that. Apart from the *Yorkshireman*, berthed alongside to have the repairs caused by the *Cedarbank* made good, which he estimated would take several days at least, their workload had slackened. By the end of August he noted 'there are days now where it is difficult to find something to write about.'

However, on 5 September he was more upbeat:

Incredible day. Decided on spur of the moment to go over to Artemis box on Goldsworthy Hill. Incredible amounts of arms and ammunition, shells and bullets, grenades lying about. Very dangerous ... Then decided to call at officers' mess of 847 Squadron to see if they needed anything, in a way of thanks for relocating Artemis.

The incredible day was followed by a 'bad night', during which the anchor dragged:

It should have been noted earlier. Not easy to find the reason as the DP was on ... Anyway we dragged 500 metres before I was called. However, easy enough to recover the position and dragged all ships back and re-anchored. We are changing an Olympus turbine engine on *Southampton*. This has never been done at sea before so everyone is a bit tense. There is no real guarantee of success and high winds don't help. Still, things calmed off in the afternoon.

He noted on the next day that the Olympus engine had been successfully installed in the *Southampton*:

They've really got on well with the work on *Southampton* and the Olympus is already fitted. They are now talking about doing engine trials alongside us – that should be interesting!

Those engine trials were duly undertaken, and with the aid of the dynamic positioning system they were held in place while the trials took place. That was another first for the ship. The *Southampton* sailed at 15.00 on the next day, and work on the *Yorkshireman* also finished with successful sea trials.

The problem with the unions, mentioned earlier, had reappeared. He called the crew together and sent a telex refuting the 'silly demands' made by the union, stating what was really wanted, which was not very different from the offer that had been made.

On 15 September the *Norland* arrived at 07.30 with the relief crew members. She:

> ... did a quick arrangement with *Yorkshireman* to get our lads over. They were all aboard by 09.30. So there will be a bit of interest getting to know the newcomers. AB B living up to reputation for drink. Within nine hours he had received his first and last warning on here. Nothing alongside now until Sunday, when *Amazon* due in.

However, this proved not to be the case, as on the next day there was:

> ... excitement with *Irishman* who said there had been an explosion under her and she was damaged and listing. She came alongside us under her own steam. Quick response by divers who were out in about 15 minutes. Preliminary survey may indicate grounding rather than explosion. Fuller dive tomorrow.

More excitement followed the next day:

> *Saxonia* came in to anchor and had two attempts, then steamed into a position with very little manoeuvring room, got beam onto 40 knots of wind on a lee shore and grounded. We went over to assist after *Yorkshireman* and *Irishman* had made fast. On a falling tide so nothing could be achieved for several hours. Divers again in operation, confirmed no fatal damage. Called in to make fast at the bow. Inept seamanship by both Stena and RN people delayed the tow, and just as it was about to occur she slid off stern first. Lot of hassle for nothing on our part.

On Sunday 19 and Monday 20 September *Diomede* left, *Amazon* came alongside, and there was an unplanned berthing of *Southampton* for repairs to an aerial. On Wednesday David Ede managed to make a reservation for a flight home on 2 October, as his relief was due to arrive on 30 September. On the 27th they sailed from Port Stanley round to Port Egmont for some rest and relaxation. They arrived in the afternoon and he:

> ... went ashore to the settlement – the Evans family. 31,000 acres with 8000 sheep and 80 cattle. Quite a pretty place but so lonely ... Good sheltered anchorage and pretty scenery – will do for a break.

On Wednesday they sailed round to Port San Carlos to take bunkers from the *British Trent*:

> Red alert at 09.00 with Argentinian plane 37 miles away. Resulted in Hercules being turned back so Bob [Bob Fitch-his relief] not arrived ... At 23.30 called out because second cook drunk – deal with him later.

Three and a half hours later:

> Called at 0300. Trouble between MN and RN catering departments, fights, knife pulled, black eyes etc. Taking statements this morning over whole incident. Arrived Berkeley Sound 07.30 to give technical assistance to *Alvega* and *British Forth*. Decided to stay the night. Much cheered by arrival of Bob Fitch, he'd had a bad journey. Problems of the night resolved. Second cook drunk given final written warning but the violence down to RN AB C, who has been charged under Naval Discipline Act with MN rating as witness.

The last entry in David Ede's diary is dated 1 October:

> Handed over pretty well everything to Bob Fitch. Will leave tomorrow, weather permitting, arriving after 13-hour flight in Hercules at Ascension Island a.m. Sunday, thence VC10 to Brize Norton arriving 20.00 Sunday. Feeling low and rather anticlimactic.

The option to purchase the *Stena Inspector* that was part of the original charter agreement was exercised by the Ministry of Defence. She became RFA *Diligence* and continued in her role as a repairs ship, at one stage spending five and a half years on deployment before returning to the United Kingdom.

The smallest ships in the Task Force

The managing director's tale

Captain Michael Lacey was the managing director of United Towing from 1982 to 1992. His account of his memories of the Falklands War sets out very clearly the involvement of the tugs and the need for them:

> At the beginning of 1982, United Towing Ltd, the Hull-based ocean towage and marine salvage company, was operating three ocean-going salvage tugs. These were *Salvageman*, *Yorkshireman* and *Irishman*.
>
> United Towing's ocean-going tug fleet had declined dramatically during the latter half of the 1970s, with the sale of a large number of ocean-going salvage tugs due to the decline in the towage market. Whilst the tug fleet had declined, it was very modern and powerful. *Yorkshireman* and *Irishman* were twin-screw sister tugs of 4380 bhp and 70 tons bollard pull, built at Cochrane Shipbuilders in Goole in 1978. Both tugs were 39.00 metres in length and 11.00 metres in beam and had a ten-man crew. *Salvageman*, an anchor-handling, ocean-towing salvage tug, had been built in Hong Kong and delivered to United Towing in 1980. She was then the most powerful tug in the UK, with 170 tons bollard pull. She was 68.25 metres in length, with a beam of 14.23 metres, and had twin screws with four main engines which produced over 11,000 bhp., with a maximum speed of 17.5 knots. She had a crew of 15, but had accommodation for 28 in total. She had two main towing winches and a large anchor-handling winch.
>
> All three tugs were registered in the port of Hull, and their crews had close connections with the city, as many of them had grandfathers, fathers, uncles, brothers, nephews and cousins who had served on United Towing tugs. In fact, during the Falklands Campaign the Bales family of Hull had a son serving on each tug, possibly the biggest

family contribution to the Task Force.

At the beginning of April 1982, *Salvageman* was in Aberdeen, where she was undergoing DOT [Department of Transport] surveys. At that time the tug was on a long-term charter to the McDermott organisation to work with their crane barge, DB 100, on operations in the North Sea. *Irishman* was about to commence the tow of a barge from Flushing in Holland to Finland, and *Yorkshireman* was working on the Magnus Project in the North Sea for the American company Brown and Root.

With the news of the invasion of the Falkland Islands on 2 April, the old hands in United Towing anticipated that the tugs would be taken up for service with the Navy, as on two previous occasions, during the 1970s, United Towing tugs had worked with the Royal Navy protecting the UK fishing fleet during the Icelandic 'Cod Wars'.

At midday on Tuesday 6 April, United Towing received a telephone call from the Shipping Policy Division of the Department of Transport advising that *Salvageman* had been requisitioned by the Ministry of Defence, and was instructed to proceed to the RN Dockyard at Portsmouth. Just over 24 hours later a further call was received advising that both *Irishman* and *Yorkshireman* were also requisitioned for service with the Royal Navy and they were also to proceed without delay to Portsmouth Dockyard.

For the operations and chartering managers in the office in Hull there followed a period of numerous telephone calls to the tugs' various charterers in Scotland, USA, Holland and Finland, explaining exactly what requisitioned meant, that the tugs' commercial commitments had come to an end for an unknown period of time and alternative towage assistance would have to be engaged.

Irishman left her tow in Flushing and was the first tug to arrive in Portsmouth on the morning of 8 April, and there then began the process of storing, bunkering and carrying out a crew change prior to departure for what at that time was to be an unknown period of service with the Royal Navy.

Yorkshireman had been towing a 400-foot offshore barge from Ardersier in Scotland to the Magnus Project site in the North Sea. She was then well north of the Shetlands, and was ordered to turn about and take the barge into Lerwick. This ultimately involved a night-time entry into Lerwick in a following gale. The tug's master, Peter Rimmer, later said it was not something he ever wanted to try again.

Salvageman arrived in Portsmouth late on 8 April. The following day a truck load of additional salvage equipment was sent from United Towing's store in Hull to be placed on board the three salvage tugs.

This equipment included additional salvage pumps for the *Irishman* and *Yorkshireman*, and a large-capacity pumping system to be loaded on *Salvageman*, as well as four large low-pressure inflatable fenders, which could be used during any ship-to-ship transfer operations.

During the course of 9 April a quantity of additional salvage equipment was loaded on board *Salvageman* by the Royal Navy. Four naval personnel, three communications and one medical, joined her, and three naval personnel, two communications and one medical, joined the *Irishman*.

In terms of preparations for the forthcoming role of the tugs, other than the loading of additional salvage equipment, the provision of communication and medical personnel, and the supply of black-out material, there was no additional work needed to be carried out on the tugs, since their role in any conflict would be virtually the same as their normal role of providing towage services and rendering salvage assistance to maritime casualties.

Food supplies came from the Royal Navy. When they

looked at the tugs' requirements one of the RN sailors suggested it was 'like weekend shopping at Sainsbury's', compared to storing a navy ship.

During the morning of Saturday 10 April, *Irishman* sailed from Portsmouth under instructions to proceed to Ascension Island in the South Atlantic. Later the same day *Salvageman* also departed Portsmouth with similar instructions to proceed to Ascension.

On Monday 12 April *Yorkshireman* arrived in Portsmouth. She began a similar process of storing, bunkering and changing the crew and also took on board additional naval personnel and specialised radio equipment. The following day *Yorkshireman* departed from Portsmouth for Ascension Island, where she arrived on 27 April.

Salvageman had reached Ascension on 22 April and was instructed to anchor off. Just over a day and a half later, *Irishman* arrived off Ascension and also anchored off. On the evening of Monday 26 April, after bunkering, *Salvageman* sailed from Ascension on passage for Tristan da Cunha, where she arrived on Sunday 2 May. However, within a few hours she was instructed to proceed immediately to South Georgia, accompanied by the naval tug RMAS *Typhoon*.

Up until 3 May, *Yorkshireman* and *Irishman* had remained off Ascension carrying out various tasks to assist the numerous Task Force ships arriving off the island. On that day both tugs sailed from Ascension for Tristan da Cunha, but the following day *Yorkshireman* suffered a main radio transmitter breakdown. However, arrangements were made for a replacement transmitter to be parachuted to the tug further down the South Atlantic, and this all went to plan.

On 6 May *Salvageman* was navigating through heavy icebergs towards South Georgia and the following evening the tug arrived at South Georgia. Having been ordered to proceed as a darkened vessel and to maintain radio silence, it became apparent that the British forces who had recaptured South Georgia were not expecting the tug, and as she slowly approached Grytviken she was challenged and ordered to identify herself and not to proceed any further without risk of being fired upon. Fortunately everything was sorted out, and the captain and RN communication personnel were sent to HMS *Endurance* for orders.

On 8 May, *Salvageman* was instructed to proceed to the assistance of HMS *Sheffield*, which had been attacked four days earlier by the Argentinian air force. Late on the 9th she arrived at the reported location of *Sheffield* but there was no sign of the vessel. She was instructed to remain in the area, pending further instructions.

On 10 May *Irishman* and *Yorkshireman* both arrived and anchored off Tristan da Cunha, where they were to spend a week, enjoying the hospitality provided by the islanders. They sailed on 16 May, under instructions to proceed to a rendezvous area 255 miles northeast of the Falklands. This area became the TARA, or 'tug and rescue area', where the tugs and various other support vessels were to maintain station as the fighting at sea, and later ashore on the Falklands, increased in intensity.

On 21 May British forces landed on the Falklands, and some three days later *Irishman* and *Yorkshireman* rendezvoused with *Salvageman* in the TARA. Late on the following day, 25 May, *Salvageman* was ordered to proceed to the assistance of *Atlantic Conveyor*, which had been struck by Argentinian Exocet missiles.

Early on the next day she approached *Atlantic Conveyor*, which was then on fire from stem to stern. However, the tug was challenged by HMS *Alacrity* and ordered to proceed back to her holding position.[3] *Irishman*

---

[3] There was no reason given for this at the time.

was then ordered to proceed to the assistance of *Atlantic Conveyor*.

So, on 27 May at 08.46, *Irishman* reached *Atlantic Conveyor* and her master, Captain Tony Allen, subsequently reported that the bow section, about one-third of the length of the vessel, had been blown off. The vessel had clearly been on fire throughout, all the accommodation section was badly burnt, the containers on the remaining foredeck were burnt out, but some looked intact. A helicopter on the afterdeck was burnt out, there was a large hole about 2 feet in diameter through the shell plates on the portside below the accommodation. The vessel had a list to starboard and was trimmed well by the stern. Smoke was still escaping from the forward end and also some from the aft end.

Nobody had been on board to make any detailed inspection due to the risk of further explosion and fire because of the nature of the cargo, including aircraft fuel and ammunition still on board the vessel. Three crewmembers, the second officer and two ABs, were placed on board the stern of the casualty to make fast a towing connection. *Irishman* was instructed to tow *Atlantic Conveyor* clear of the total exclusion zone, but at that time no destination was given.

The initial towing connection subsequently parted and the two ABs went back on the casualty and another towing connection was established. The tug then continued towing the stern half of *Atlantic Conveyor* in the direction of South Georgia.

The tow was being carried out in thick fog. At about 00.45 hours on 28 May the tug experienced a sudden heavy jolt on the towing gear and it was clear it had parted again. The radar was switched on and a target was spotted 1½ miles away, but on closing that area and using searchlights it was found that this was a floating container. There was no sign of *Atlantic Conveyor*, which had clearly sunk.

Subsequently the two ABs, Gary Bales and Dennis Betts, were each awarded the British Empire Medal for their bravery in twice boarding the *Atlantic Conveyor* to establish the towing connection.

During the remaining period of the conflict, the three tugs continued to provide assistance to a number of Task Force vessels. This included recovering one of the *Saxonia*'s anchor cables, together with thirteen shackles of cable, picking up Special Air Service troops and their equipment, who had parachuted into the sea from a Hercules close by *Irishman*, as well as various other activities with the Navy.

On 14 June the Argentinian forces in the Falklands surrendered, but the tugs remained in the TARA.

The next significant event for the tugs was on 17 June when *Salvageman* proceeded, together with HMS *Endurance*, the frigate HMS *Yarmouth* and the RFA Tanker *Olmeda*, to the South Sandwich Islands for the recapture of Southern Thule. This island had in fact been occupied by Argentinian forces since 1976, and the decision had been made to deal with this long-outstanding matter. This operation provided an unusual involvement for the captain of *Salvageman*, Alan Stockwell, as he and the captain of *Olmeda* were invited to be witnesses to the surrender ceremony on board HMS *Endurance*. Captain Stockwell was picked up from the deck of *Salvageman* by a helicopter from HMS *Endurance* but, unfortunately for him, the winching system failed and he had to be transported between the two vessels suspended from the helicopter's lifting wire in temperatures many degrees below zero. On arrival on HMS *Endurance* they almost had to chip him away from the lifting wire.

The previous day, *Irishman* had arrived in Port Stanley, where she remained for a few days before being instructed to proceed to Port San Carlos. *Salvageman* returned to South Georgia with HMS *Endurance*. In the meantime, *Irishman* was instructed to proceed to Fox Bay and engage in salvage operations on the Argentinian auxiliary vessel *Bahia Buen Suceso*.

Salvageman was then instructed to proceed to Grytviken to carry out salvage operations on the Argentinian submarine *Santa Fe*. This submarine had been attacked by a helicopter from HMS *Endurance* during the operations to recapture South Georgia and was lying alongside the only jetty in Grytviken in a partially sunken condition with only her conning tower and bow above water. The salvage operations on this vessel continued for the next fifteen days, with the crew of *Salvageman* assisting a team of Royal Navy divers and personnel from HMS *Endurance*. These were carried out in the most inhospitable sub-zero conditions and the submarine itself was flooded with seawater which was contaminated with fuel oil, rotten food, sewage, battery acid and leaking explosives. On 14 July *Santa Fe* was refloated and taken by *Salvageman*, assisted by *Yorkshireman*, to be beached approximately 2 miles from Grytviken.

Salvageman and *Yorkshireman* then proceeded on passage to Port Stanley, where they arrived on 19 July. *Yorkshireman* and *Irishman* were then based in Port Stanley harbour assisting various Task Force vessels, whilst the *Salvageman* remained in Falkland Sound and the San Carlos/Fox Bay area carrying out diving operations with the RN on HMS *Ardent* and HMS *Antelope*, which had been lost during hostilities. *Salvageman* was also engaged in assisting the support vessel *Stena Seaspread*, which was carrying out other diving operations on HMS *Sheffield* and HMS *Coventry*, which had both been sunk off the Falklands.

On 28 September, *Irishman* was the first United Towing tug to leave the Falklands, and she arrived back in the UK on 29 October. Following a refit and the installation of satellite communications, a larger workboat, and a more powerful crane, United Towing was again approached by the Department of Transport Shipping Policy Division, who requested that *Irishman* be chartered to them for further service in the Falklands – and so, after a short period of time in UK waters, the tug returned to the Falkland Islands.

Yorkshireman arrived back in Hull at the end of 1983, but *Salvageman* did not return to the UK until 22 June 1984, some 2 years and 3 months after her departure. During her extended time in the Falklands, she had returned to South Georgia and carried out further salvage operations on the *Santa Fe* with the Royal Navy, as it had been concluded that the location in which the submarine was lying might prove tempting to passing shipping or yachtsmen, and therefore the submarine should be taken out to sea and sunk. However, whilst she was under tow to what was to be her final resting place, and during an attempt to reduce the list on the submarine, she sank prematurely, not out at sea as had been intended. As a consequence, following a major refit in the UK, *Salvageman* was chartered back to the Royal Navy for a period of 6 months in October 1984 and returned to South Georgia with an RN salvage vessel and a large naval salvage team, and on this occasion the *Santa Fe* was raised, taken out to sea and scuttled in well over 1000 metres depth of water.

Looking back over nearly 30 years there are still some abiding memories:

- The way the country pulled together and achieved so much in so little time.
- Discovering that 'stuffed' actually meant STUFT – 'ships taken up from trade'.
- The sinking of HMS *Sheffield*, which made everyone realise that this was no longer a game.
- Being called to a meeting at the old General Council of British Shipping in St Mary Axe, to

listen to the MOD advising that shipping losses were likely, that they would try to prevent any loss becoming a news item for 24 hours, and that each shipping company should nominate a 24-hour contact to receive any such news.

- The incredible homecoming scenes in Southampton, Portsmouth and elsewhere.
- Receiving a bill from the NAAFI, months, if not years, after it was all over, for £28,000 for victualling supplied to the three tugs over a prolonged period of time!
- United Towing's overall involvement in the Falklands Task Force and in the years that followed.

7

The RFA ships

Olmeda

Sir Lancelot

Olmeda

The *Olmeda* was a fast fleet tanker of 33,250 deadweight tons with a design speed of 21 knots from a steam turbine engine. She was built at the Swan Hunter yard on the River Tyne and commissioned in November 1964. She had the ability to carry furnace fuel oil, which she had on board for the *Hermes*, diesel fuel, which was for the more modern frigates and destroyers, and aviation fuel, all at the same time. She also had a flight deck and the ability to operate helicopters. She took with her to the South Atlantic 'A' Flight of 824 Squadron, Fleet Air Arm, which comprised two Sea King Mark II helicopters.

John Kelly was her first officer, joining her on 26 February 1982. Apart from his Master Mariner's certificate he also was a qualified flight deck officer, in charge of the helicopter operations on board and the smooth and successful operation of the flight deck, which was at the after end of the ship. This was also his position at action stations, so that his view of proceedings was restricted to what was happening more or less astern of the ship. His flying diary records briefly the daily events relating to his responsibility in relation to the flight deck, and the diary is therefore taken up with technical matters relating to that function.

Jeremy Carew, as chief officer and therefore the ship's second in command, issued daily orders relating to the running of the ship and crew. The remarks that followed the times and events for the day occasionally throw light on the events beyond the official language of the daily orders.

Taken together, the two documents give a different and focused view of life on board. There is little information as to the ship's location on a daily basis; however, this has been interpolated, where appropriate, from other sources.

John Kelly's entry on 5 April, therefore, simply says 'Sail Devonport'. The daily orders show that the crew started work at 08.00 and they were due to sail at 16.15. Jeremy Carew's remarks relate to the last-minute details before sailing, but he comments 'expect anything at any time, we will probably be still loading as we slip.'

Three days later, on 8 April, John Kelly noted 'no flying due to inclement weather'. The weather may have been too inclement for helicopter operations, but they were able to replenish the HMS *Alacrity* and *Antelope*, the former becoming a regular 'customer' for fuel from the *Olmeda*. The next day, Good Friday, the weather improved and helicopter flying recommenced. By Easter Saturday, when they replenished *Invincible*, the last remark in the daily orders for that day is 'there is no truth in the rumour that the ChOff [chief officer] is judging Easter Bonnet parade on Sunday.'

On Friday 15 April, as they crossed the equator, captain's rounds was held at 10.00. There was no ceremony for crossing the line, but the remarks for the day contained the following:

King Neptune sends the following message: 'Being otherwise occupied mustering my aquatic forces against Argentina, I shall be unable to visit your vessel today. However, I have ordered that all you lovely mortals that are crossing my line for the first time be issued with a certificate countersigned by your master Captain Overbury. I shall appear in all splendour on your way back to see that justice is done. Nimph [*sic*] has delivered my trident to you as a sign of good sailing'. Therefore could any person that has not crossed the line before, hand their name into the purser's office by 10.00 this morning.

Following the captain's rounds, the next day's remarks note:

1. Captain's rounds were below standard and an improvement to our usual standard is required next week
...

and:

3. There is no truth in the rumour that we are now designated FA(RT), i.e. Fast Auxiliary (Replenishment Tanker).

The number of replenishments at sea that they undertook was increasing. On 18 April there were six, including both *Hermes* and *Invincible*: as the daily orders said, 'stand by for zero minutes warning to RAS, RAS, RAS.'

In addition to RASing, *Olmeda* was also 'vertreping' (moving dry stores by helicopter), so on 19 April twelve loads went to *Stromness* and five to *Antelope*. This continued in the following days, supplying *Hermes, Invincible, Arrow, Glasgow* and *Coventry*.

On Friday 23 April the chief officer's remarks noted, 'as from 20.00 tonight, we are now in all aspects ready for war.' During that day they had replenished *Hermes, Invincible* and three other ships. They were also transferring weapons to *Hermes* by 'vertrep'. Progress to the war zone continued, and the next day the remarks noted that 'tin hats are to be carried'. This was the precursor to meeting the Battle Group, which they did at midnight on the next day. This coincided with worsening weather, and flying was halted at 20.15 because the flight deck was out of bounds for safety reasons.

On that day an air crewman was lost when a Sea King was forced to ditch. A combined rescue operation was mounted by *Olmeda, Resource,* and *Yarmouth*. John Kelly's diary notes briefly, 'SAR in action ... *Resource* has been ordered to recover wreckage. Pilot survived. Crewman missing PD [presumed dead]. Stood down at 03.00.'

May started with a full programme of RASs. On the 2nd they replenished eleven ships in one day, and on the 5th they carried out a further ten. Jeremy Carew's remarks on the 4th warned 'stand by to RAS, RAS, RAS'. John Kelly's log notes:

> p.m. – HMS *Sheffield* attacked and damaged. Submarine created diversion – that was it. [Depth charges] dropped – nothing, however first time weapons dropped in war by helicopter from an RFA.

The continuous action gave Jeremy Carew little time to write his daily orders, which became very brief; on that day the remarks noted two comments relating to air-raid warnings and the necessity to be appropriately dressed at all times, with sleeves down, and anti-flash hoods and helmets to be carried at all times. After the attack on HMS *Sheffield*, it was reported that the Argentinian aircraft fired two Exocet missiles but only one hit home. The destination of the other was a mystery, but John Kelly, from his position on the aft flight deck, was one of the very few who saw it splash down about a mile astern of them, although he did not recognise it as such at the time.

On 7 May they rendezvoused with RFAs *Appleleaf*, *Blue Rover* and *Fort Austin*, and replenished their cargo tanks from the RFA *Appleleaf*, which was one of the RFA freighting tankers, in a transfer referred to as a 'pump-over', in bad weather. During that day they also carried out five RASs and were operating helicopters at the same time. The RASs finished at 01.30 the following day; helicopter operations had finished an hour and a quarter previously.

There is some confusion in the accounts of the events of 11 May. Geoff Puddefoot records that *British Esk* carried out a pump-over to the *Olmeda*;[1] the chief officer's orders note that there were planned RASs to *Brilliant* and *Glasgow*; the first officer's log notes that the weather was bad with force 8/9 gales and there was no flying. The ship's replenishment programme, which shows a complete list of all replenishments and pump-overs undertaken by *Olmeda*, records that there were no RASs carried out on that day, probably as a result of the weather conditions, and that the *British Esk* did not pump over to the *Olmeda* on any day in May, although on the 27th the *British Tay* did.[2]

The bad weather continued for several days. It had abated to some degree on the 15th and flying resumed late on that day, but clearly the conditions were still poor, as early on the 16th one of the Sea Kings landed heavily enough to burst a tyre and gouge a hole in the flight deck.

The proposed replenishments and those that actually took place differed widely, but between 13 and 16 May they undertook fifteen RASs, eight of them on the 16th. The surge on that day was the result of the weather abating, and again it was a case of 'stand by to RAS, RAS, RAS', as Jeremy Carew noted. The changes in the RAS programme led to a comment on the 17th that 'it is not being buggered about, it's called being flexible'; on that day they carried out a seven-hour pump-over from *Appleleaf* and replenished *Hermes*, *Invincible* and two

---

[1] G. Puddefoot, *No Sea too Rough*. London, 2007, 106.
[2] Subsequent conversation with Jeremy Carew clarified this. The logs were not accurate. Ships arrived and were refuelled as required, and the names were not always accurately recorded.

frigates. The heavy landing of the helicopter on the 16th meant that it required major checks. Once these were completed, they were in action virtually all day, every day, for the next week.

Both John Kelly and Jeremy Carew make reference on 21 May to the invasion. John Kelly noted 'airborne again at 11.00 for SuScreen [submarine screen] during Falkland Islands landing'. Jeremy Carew noted that 'the invasion started early today. Stand by to RAS and fly at very short notice.' The next day Jeremy Carew commented, 'the object of yesterday's operation was to land our troops and consolidate in the Falklands. That operation was 100 per cent successful.' The upbeat tone continued on the next day: 'It would appear that the only Argy bit of kit we didn't clobber was the partridge in the pear tree.'

The mood was broken on 25 May, which was the Argentinian National Day. John Kelly described it as a 'black day – *Atlantic Conveyor* sunk as well as *Coventry*.' Information on the two ships was noted in the daily remarks for the next two days. However, on 28 May the flight deck log notes '*Olmeda* detached from TG [Task Group] for weekend off.' This was described in the chief officer's remarks merely as 'RAS free maintenance period'. On Monday 31 May they were back to work, but the replenishment programme for June was much less than for May: 93 replenishments were carried out in May but only 25 in June. They were advised to stand by for a heavy RAS programme but the numbers did not appear: there were three the next day and only two the day after that.

The month started with a slightly bizarre item being found. The ship's office came across a small Austrian smoked cheese in the mail bag. Its owner was invited to reclaim it.

The helicopters were showing signs of wear. On 11 June the gearbox seized on one, requiring major repairs, and three days later the sonar on the other ceased operating. On 16 June John Kelly noted that the one working Sea King:

> ... with one crew departed for stay in HMS *Invincible*. Deck very nearly unusable ... The bridge just do not appreciate the danger involved.... On the points raised above, the limit of tyre adhesion is the one that concerns me.

On the day before it had been decided that the occupation of the island of South Thule by the Argentinians was to be terminated, so *Olmeda*, HMS *Yarmouth*, HMS *Endurance* and the tug *Salvageman* were deputed to carry out the task. As the chief officer's remarks explained it to the crew:

> We are going to collect Argies from South Thule (whether they want to come or not) ... We will accommodate the Argies from South Thule (don't know where we are taking them as yet).

They had embarked 80 Royal Marines to help them with the task and arrived there on 20 June. The remarks for that day are extensive. John Kelly's flight deck log remarks:

> Long day on duty (deck) from 0900 to 1930 with just 20 minutes off for lunch. Had to use KILFROST AL-34 [anti-freeze] on the deck to keep it clear; it took three applications. C/S 55 [one of the two Sea Kings] carried 24 troops (total of 28 in the aircraft), two trips. Very light on fuel. Icing conditions serious for some of the other aircraft. Assault over, prisoners and troops return to *Olmeda*. Remain on duty as the captain had to go to *Endurance* for the surrender ceremony.

The chief officer's daily orders give a clue of the works that went on to receive and accommodate the prisoners of war:

> 0800 – Carpenter to hangar ... to make and position 10-foot table
> 0800 – Deck store keeper provide six buckets, brooms, dustpan and brushes
> 0800 – Assistant purser provide pens, pencils and 400 labels in hangar
> 0830 – Accommodation shift for Marines in hangar
> a.m. – Fit alarm in hangar

His remarks include:

> Today's mission is to recapture South Thule. Timings and events will be super flexy. *Olmeda* will embark the Argy prisoners, who will be detained in the hangar. We will be

very crowded on the way back ... Toilet facilities will be strained.

The following day's remarks include the comment:

The Union Flag, M Coy [Royal Marines] and the RFA ensign fly over South Thule.

They proceeded back to South Georgia, where the prisoners were disembarked. Despite preparing for large numbers of prisoners, only one civilian and nine military personnel were captured. The operation to recapture South Thule had been carried out just in time, as a few days later the island was completely surrounded by thick pack ice.

By the time they left South Georgia the daily orders were able to remark, 'We are homeward bound but don't know as yet which one. Land's End for orders.' They returned to a more relaxed routine very quickly, with the crew bars reverting to normal opening times and mealtimes at set hours.

Flying was continuing on 26 June, the stores being flown in from other ships. John Kelly noted:

Loads from HMS *Invincible* (six engines), One sonar support frame weight 4000 lb lost from helo. It would probably have been too big for the flight deck anyway.

After that comment his diary becomes very brief, as activities diminished until the flight disembarked to RN Culdrose on 10 July, and his duties as flight deck officer were little exercised. The chief officer's daily orders also became more brief, showing, for example, orders for the return of anti-flash gear, helmets and survival suits and the returning of the ship to its normal clean state.

Eventually, on 3 July, they learnt that they were to return to Plymouth. A week later, the arrangements for their arrival on the 12th were set out, instructing the crew to collect clean new boiler suits to wear on arrival, and that all officers on the upper deck were to wear caps. The programme for that day noted that at 09.15 the pilot boarded, and at 10.35:

Alongside No. 1 jetty (starboard side to): Marine band, port admiral, families, TV etc.

After their return, Jeremy Carew received a letter from the MNAOA (Merchant Navy and Airline Officers Association) enclosing a survey which the government had asked them to undertake on the lessons to be drawn from the Merchant Navy's role in the conflict. The last question was headed 'own experience'. Jeremy Carew wrote:

> Any RFA officer who feels that he should be given the option as to whether he wishes to do his duty (for which he has been trained all these years) should be at the *top* of the list for redundancy. The RFA during Operation Corporate was not asked to do any more than we do on exercises. Hours worked were in most cases longer than normal. My job was easy in general due to the high morale of our ratings and their proficiency at RAS.

Jeremy Carew spent his entire career with the Royal Fleet Auxiliary. In the course of a very extensive interview with the author he discussed his experiences in the Falklands at the time of the conflict:

> Yes, I was down there as chief officer on a ship called the *Olmeda*, which was a replenishment tanker with a helicopter. We had two helicopters. We did 185 replenishments. We took fuel from the *British Wye*, the *British Esk*, all of the BP River class. We took fuel ten times from them. We used to pull out of the area, go well out of the threat. We put our rigs across to them. It didn't take a long time to put a reception hose on, they had the bell end, which they received at the manifold amidships somewhere. They had had a pad eye welded there somewhere to help. We had some chief officers sent to them so they would know what was expected. The trouble was we had to be careful that people weren't washed off. The seas would break over the deck. Under 10 knots it was difficult to steer, and over 12 knots there was too much water coming on. So if you wanted 10,000 tonnes of fuel we're talking about 10 hours alongside, which is a bloody long time just to keep station on a ship.

All the BP ships had to do was just steer a straight course. Normally, when a naval ship comes up, because we are the issuing ship we are the guide and he keeps station on us, but when we came to the BP ship, she was the issuing ship so all she had to do was just steer a straight course. They were about the same size as us.

One of the reasons that we won the war down there is that we kept Zulu time. We stayed on GMT. So at seven o'clock in the morning it was pitch dark. By the time it got light we had got into a natural rhythm, by the time it got light it was midday and we'd all been up and got sorted. Chico, across there, gets out of his bed and into his aeroplane at 10 o'clock his time. We'd had five hours of day before the buggers started coming to attack us. It was the only way to do it so everybody worked the same time schedule so that there was no confusion over timeshift, it was always done on Zulu time, so you always know that it is GMT.

Sir Lancelot

Sir Lancelot was the first of the six 'Knights of the Round Table' class of landing ship logistic (LSL), which had been built in the 1960s for the Army to a design agreed by the Ministry of Transport (as it was then). The design was very specialised; they could carry 340 troops (or nearly twice that for a short distance), 16 battle tanks, 34 vehicles and 150 tons of fuel or ammunition. Flight decks on the main deck and after deck gave helicopter capability. As a single deck cargo, instead of tanks and vehicles they could carry up to 20 helicopters. They had bow and stern ramps, to allow a roll-on/roll-off capability and, given a suitably inclined beach, could discharge straight off the forward ramp onto the beach. In the 1970s the management and operation of the ships, which had been undertaken by the British India Steam Navigation Company, passed to the Royal Fleet Auxiliary.

The chief officer's diary

David Gerrard was the chief officer on *Sir Lancelot*, and he subsequently put together a diary of events, based on his recollections and from the records that had been kept by the master (Captain C. Purtcher-Wydenbruck OBE RFA).

On 2 April 1982 *Sir Lancelot* returned to Marchwood Military Port, in Southampton Water, from Zeebrugge, where she had been with *Sir Percivale*. The latter returned to Marchwood the next day. The appropriate stores for their destination in the South Atlantic were ordered and loading commenced the next day, continuing for the next three days. They embarked over 300 troops, including units of the Commando Logistics Regiment and the First Raiding Squadron, together with vehicles, ammunition and stores.

On 6 April David Gerrard notes 'Sailed Marchwood, overloaded by 13 inches, to rendezvous with the Amphibious Task Group off Plymouth.' For the next eleven days they were on passage to Ascension Island in company with the other LSLs, the store ship RFA *Stromness*, the tanker RFA *Plumleaf*, and the naval assault ships HMS *Fearless* and HMS *Intrepid*.

On arrival at Ascension Island, specialist troops joined the ship to man the air defence weapons; a Bofors anti-aircraft gun was fitted and the ship was supplied with Blowpipe anti-aircraft missile launchers and machine guns. They were at Ascension until 30 April, and, after loading 500 tons of fresh water from *Fort Toronto*, they sailed with the other LSLs, initially under the protection of HMS *Antelope*. They proceeded south for the next two weeks. On 10 May, a problem arose: 'The main boiler steam coil failed. No evaporating capacity. Supply of fresh water, always a problem, now even more critical.' As they approached the total exclusion zone off the Falklands on 19 May, they received supplies of food from *Stromness*. On the next day he notes, 'Orders for the landings received.'

So on 21 May they:

> ... entered Falkland Sound shortly before dawn and passed through the later stages of the delayed assault waves [of landing craft] to anchor in San Carlos Water at 11.25 GMT. Uniquely, the *Sir Lancelot* was not to leave here until 25 of

> June ... Air attacks begin early afternoon and continue until dusk. The targets are the escorts.

Two days later he notes:

> Weather fine. Continued discharge. Air attacks p.m. *Antelope* collected two UXB [unexploded bombs] and anchored nearby. A spectacular view of the demise after one bomb exploded whilst 'our' RE [Royal Engineer] team attempted to defuse it. The anchorage is re-arranged.

The next day, after she had moved to a different anchorage, the war came to *Sir Lancelot*:

> At 13.45 a wave of three Skyhawks approaching down the valley from the south drop six 1000 lb bombs, one of which came inboard having bounced off the water. Entering the starboard side ... it [was] deflected by the deckhead, fractured the fire main ... and cable runs ... into the engine room casing, destroying generator exhaust ... ends up in film locker. No casualties ... Resulting damage: no fire main, no power to bridge/radio room, decision made to evacuate ship ... Ship's company and remaining embarked force (total 240) were taken ashore ... at 15.00. Welcomed, fed and watered ... they awaited a decision on their future. None having arrived by nightfall, the ship's company bedded down in the disused refrigeration plant.

Early the next morning the crew were transferred to RFA *Stromness*, except for the Chinese crew, who apart from two, declined to move; they were moved later in the day 'by military methods'. No further explanation as to those methods is given.

The air attacks continued. He records:

> Probably this is when *Sir Lancelot* was hit for the second time ... she was also strafed by 20 mm cannon.

As the *Sir Galahad* also had an unexploded bomb on board, her crew was also on the *Stromness*. As her bomb was more accessible it was decided to deal with it first:

> So the *Galahad*'s officers and four 'volunteers' from *Lancelot* (chief officer [David Gerrard], chief and third

engineer officers and first electrical officer) crossed to HMS *Fearless*.

The crews remained on *Stromness*, who left the immediate area. On 27 May:

> The four return to *Lancelot*. Lt Bruen [RE] secured the bomb. Engineers start generator. Fridges saved. Chief officer weighed anchor and ship towed ... to safer anchorage. It is observed that considerable looting of MoD stores and personal effects has occurred. Some of the latter were later recovered.

No indication of the likely culprits is given. The next day the work continued to remove the bomb, with the Royal Engineer bomb disposal team helped by the four officers where possible, the chief officer cooking meals. By 10.00 on 29 May the bomb was lowered into the water. The repairs continued, and by 2 June:

> Some cargo was discharged ... accommodation provided to numerous persons with convincing reasons for their presence. Chief officer resigned as cook.

Whether the increased numbers on board prompted this decision is not made clear. The remainder of the crew returned the next day.

The mechanical repairs were completed on 5 June, but the ship was not seaworthy. She became a base for 22 SAS Regiment, and three squadrons of that regiment took up residence on board. Presumably as a result of the influx of troops, he notes that on the 7th, 'an acute shortage of fresh water forces a tour of the anchorage begging from any ship with water to spare.'

A week later the ceasefire came into operation. A Royal Fleet Auxiliary ensign was hoisted on Twelve O'Clock Mountain overlooking Port Stanley. The *Sir Lancelot* remained in San Carlos Water, 'scrounging water, fuel and food from any available source'. The *Stena Seaspread* came alongside to carry out permanent repairs, following which, after 36 days in San Carlos Water, she sailed for Port Stanley.

July started with *Sir Lancelot* in Port Stanley, where she was discharging and unloading. This was followed by a voyage around the coast collecting various equipment, both British and Argentinian, together with a consignment of wool from the local sheep farmers. Arriving back in Port Stanley on 18 July, she discharged over 500 bales of wool, and received the replacement steam coil for her boiler to allow the supply of fresh water to resume. While there they also went 'sight-seeing ashore in "acquired" Mercedes G wagon'. On 24 July he writes, 'Loading for UK. Obliged to discharge Mercedes!'

Two days later they sailed for the UK via Ascension Island, dumping 25 tons of Argentinian ammunition overboard in deep water on the way. They arrived in Portsmouth on 18 August.

The *Sir Lancelot* stayed in service with the Royal Fleet Auxiliary for a further seven years before being sold. Subsequently she had a varied career, including being a cross-channel ferry, a floating casino in Cape Town, and a further eleven years in naval service with the Singaporean Navy. She was eventually scrapped in 2008.

8

RRS *Bransfield*

Bransfield was the 'odd one out'. Because of her particular role, she was employed almost solely in the Southern Ocean. Owned and operated by the British Antarctic Survey, based at Cambridge, she was registered at Stanley and had a Falkland Island crew.

She was built by Robb Caledon Shipbuilders of Leith, purpose-built and strengthened for ice operations, and launched in 1970. From then until 1999 she was the main supply ship for the British Antarctic Survey and also carried out some research. She was of 4816 gross tons, with twin diesel electric engines with a maximum endurance of 90 days before refuelling. She had a crew of 37 and could carry 58 passengers.

Bransfield was not part of Operation Corporate, nor was she taken up from trade, but at the end of March 1982 she was on passage from Stanley to Punta Arenas, in southern Chile, thereby finding herself close to the Argentinian fleet on the morning of the invasion. She was the first official source to advise the British government of the fall of Stanley and the capture of the governor. After that, she returned to her duties in the Antarctic and then returned to the United Kingdom via South Georgia. At that time the naturalists and film-makers Cindy Buxton and Annie Price were ashore in South Georgia filming, and a decision had to be made as to whether they would be recovered by the Royal Navy or by the *Bransfield*. As it was considered that the operation would put the *Bransfield* in too much danger, she returned to the United Kingdom, arriving at Southampton on the same day that *QE2* sailed for South Georgia.

Feelings among the Falkland Island crew on the *Bransfield* ran very high, as they felt they should have been helping to defend their homes, and they were close to mutiny. Shortly afterwards the Falkland newspaper *Penguin News*[1] reported that:

> According to a British newspaper, the crew of the RRS *Bransfield*, which includes a number of Falkland Islanders, attempted to mutiny when they heard of the Argentine

---

[1] *Penguin News* 16 July 1982, No. 21, 4.

invasion. Led by Falklander Michael Allan they demanded to see Captain Stuart Lawrence at 2 a.m. when the ship was just 60 miles south of Stanley. The crew demanded that the captain turn the ship around and sail into Port Stanley to help the Falklanders. For three hours the rebel delegation and the captain talked and Lawrence finally convinced them there was nothing that they could do. 'It would,' he said 'have been an embarrassment to the British government if we had been taken and held hostage. We heard news of the invasion over Falkland radio and both myself and the crew were in tears. We were staggered and a real tide of emotion swept through the ship'. Leader of the rebel crew and scientists Michael Allan said: 'We wanted to go back to Stanley with all flags flying. We all felt like fighting and helping our families and friends. I suppose we could have rammed an Argentine ship or scuttled the *Bransfield* in the Narrows. But the main thing was to show the islanders that they were not alone. The old man was pretty cool about it. He sat there sipping brandy and calmed us all down.' As the Task Force headed south, the *Bransfield*, or '*Branny*' as she is affectionately known in the Falklands, slipped out of the immediate area and continued to send back vital information about the situation. Captain Lawrence said 'it was the most useful thing we could do in the circumstances.'

A diary covering the period from 27 March to 9 April was written by an unnamed member of the crew shortly after the events. It was lent to the author by Captain Lawrence, in whose possession it was, to use for the book. It gives a clear picture of the feelings of the crew in that period.

29 March. With *Endurance* having been diverted to South Georgia, RRS *John Biscoe* was requested to take on board the normal yearly relief contingent of 40 Royal Marines at Montevideo and to return to Stanley with them. At 1800 she arrived in port. I went out to the *Biscoe* and had a

hasty conversation with the captain and catering officer before returning ashore along with all the Marines at 2000. The *Biscoe* sailed for England at 2200. We were due to sail for Punta Arenas at the same time to collect important generator spares being flown out for Signy. We did not sail on account of malfunctioning radar.

30 March. Both radars working satisfactorily by the morning but to take advantage of favourable tides in the Magellan Straits it was decided to delay sailing until the afternoon with the advantage of receiving mail on the incoming flight to Stanley in the afternoon. News from South Georgia still indicates a deadlock but Argentina now has three ships in the area. We set sail at 18.00 hours into strong winds and high seas. It was considered sailing north around the islands to shelter from the weather but decided to travel southern route as normal. (Hindsight: if we had gone north we could well have encountered advance units of the invasion fleet.)

31 March. A terrible night, only managed four hours sleep. In the morning the weather was even worse. That did not stop an Argentinian plane circling us twice. Why? We know now. Strong head seas; the weather improved somewhat during the afternoon and evening.

1 April. A calm day steaming up the Magellan Straits. In a phone call to our agents in Punta Arenas we were told that they would bring out spares by road to the pilot boat at Possession Bay, thus saving us an additional six hours steaming to Punta and six back. At 17.15 the pilot boat came out as we arrived so there was no delay and with the passing on board of the package and a wave we were on our way again. A glorious sunset with the fires of burning gas on the offshore oil rigs as a foreground did nothing to alleviate the growing feeling of alarm aroused by the radio news concerning the Falklands. First real alarm to myself was at 21.00. Britain calls for an immediate meeting of the UN Security Council – tomorrow could be too late. Reports

that the entire Argentine fleet has set sail, that all army leave has been cancelled. By 01.00 when it was reported that ... there would be a dawn invasion of Falklands I could stand it no longer. Now, one week later, I can see what a futile and dangerous course it would have been to take but until 02.30 from 01.15, when I went and woke him up, I implored Stuart (captain) to change course and head for the Falklands. My main reasoning was that the islanders, particularly our friends, would never believe, if they were invaded, that we had gone away and deserted them in their hour of need. I said better to risk the ship being seized than have such a feeling of shame. Anyhow it would be far from definite that they would touch our ship, as if they did it would certainly escalate matters. No matter what I said though, Stuart simply would not believe an invasion was possible. I went to bed full of foreboding.

2 April. At 06.05 I was woken by Stuart who in a broken voice between sobs said that a report had just been picked up on Falkland Island Radio service that landing craft were entering Stanley harbour. The invasion was a fact. Although a week has passed it still seems so unbelievable that all this ever took place. Our people, who only three days before we had been working and socialising with, are fighting for their lives. After hastily dressing I arrived in a stunned radio room. It was there I spent an anguished day hanging on every word that came in from Stanley, Grytviken and London ... It was not until two hours after a truce had been called that the BBC announced the Falklands were invaded. We seemed to be almost the only link with the UK ... To add to the feeling of unreality one had only to look out of the window to be dazzled by brilliant sunshine and the sight of Argentinian mountains on the horizon ... I still wonder what would have happened if we had gone all the way up to Punta ... On our return we would have been 12 hours later, entering the Atlantic past Argentinian Dungeness almost at the moment of

invasion!! When the final reports of the day had been gleaned the debating around the ship and the drinking began [and] feelings ran very high, dangerously so, especially with the Falkland crew and some of the youngsters. I must admit my feelings were as strong as theirs, though mutiny and charging to Stanley now the place has fallen, would have achieved only disastrous results. I fell asleep in Stuart's cabin after he succeeded in calming things down and I finally went to bed at 05.30.

3 April. A rough day weather wise as we cross Drake Passage and a rougher day news wise. Stanley radio can't be believed now it's in enemy hands, two radio hams are still getting news out though. Reports of overnight sniping and mopping-up operations do nothing to ease one's mind, nor the fact that the four British journalists in Stanley have all been evicted from the colony … The BBC state in the evening that the enemy claim to have taken Grytviken. Other reports of Stanley being turned into a fortress with reinforcements arriving by air every hour and ships offloading many armoured vehicles and supplies. Another night of speculation, concern and worry.

4 April. I still wake up stunned at the thought of what has happened. I have the lust for vengeance but still feel shattered. BBC confirmed that Grytviken fell although the Marines put up a fight, shooting down a helicopter and badly damaging a Corvette with an anti-tank gun before surrendering. Hurray … We arrived at the American base Palmer Station at 15.00 …

5 April. While the fleet steam out from Portsmouth we departed from Palmer at 07.00 for Faraday. The weather remained the same as for the past two days: gales, snow, rough seas, fog, poor visibility, as depressing as the situation, but that does not dampen our spirits. We arrived off Faraday at 11.10. Strong winds and a great deal of brash ice made it very difficult to get into the base … The weather was so bad that we sailed for Signy at 18.30 …

Our first instructions yesterday were that from Faraday and then Signy we were to steam 200 miles east of the South Sandwich Islands then head north. Now we have been instructed to wait in Signy until further notice. Personally I would prefer to stay down here in the area until the enemy have been kicked out of the Falklands and South Georgia. I would say the majority on board feel the same.

6 April. A really violent night with only the heaviest sleepers getting anything like a sleep. Amazingly with not more than a maximum of four hours sleep any one night for the past week I do not feel particularly exhausted – dazed yes. The days go by with the continual quest for news of the situation. Cursing the radio officer whenever his transmissions blot out the BBC, which is only too frequent, and everyone stops work and hangs on every word when a news broadcast is audible ... On board the ship a non-event day steaming up the Bransfield Straits. The seas are somewhat less, but the low cloud and very poor visibility continue. Who knows? It may be to our advantage.

7 April. A quiet day if that's an expression that can be used at such a time ... We continue to roll steadily along at slow speed so as to arrive in Signy tomorrow.

8 April. A day to be utterly ashamed of. All ship's personnel have now been given the daily situation report which, full praise to him, Stuart has been so good at but I am the only other one to be a party to the shameful knowledge that Her Majesty's Ship *Endurance* our sole military presence DEPARTED THESE WATERS FOR ENGLAND TWO DAYS AGO. Rule Bloody Britannia. If they were not able to get out our field parties from South Georgia at least she could have made an attempt instead of leaving them totally in the lurch. Now I know the experience of being totally physically sick. If that's not enough we have been ordered to complete the relief of

Signy then set course 200 miles south of the South Sandwich Islands then east, north and shamefully head for England. The only way our captain can persuade POSSIBLY the authorities to change their minds about ourselves is if we have 100 per cent backing for his request to stay down here. Unfortunately at least 5 per cent of ship's personnel are more concerned about their summer holidays than their pride of being British and remaining to give at least moral backing to our stranded compatriots. Today we arrived after a very rough night, yet again, at Signy at midday. The weather was too rough to work cargo. Please God that it may continue for the next two weeks.

9 April. Well, maybe someone somewhere heard my plaintive plea for bad weather as with 30–40 knot winds all day increasing to 70 in the evening it was impossible to work any cargo at all. That's one more day in which our instructions might possibly be changed. To my disgust there is a minority of 5 per cent in favour of running for home when the crunch comes.

The *Bransfield*'s subsequent movements were described by her captain, Stuart Lawrence:

After the invasion we visited the Antarctic Peninsula as planned, and then our station in the South Orkneys, before standing off South Georgia whilst the decision was made as to whether we should uplift field parties dotted around the island including Cindy Buxton and Annie Price who were ashore filming 'Wild Life'. In the event it was considered too dangerous and we were routed via the mid-Atlantic back to the UK, arriving in Southampton on the day the *QE2* sailed south. This inevitably meant that we were inundated with the world's press, such that I was unable to leave the wheelhouse for about four hours after docking. Their presence also explains how the story of the 'mutiny' came to be published.

Bransfield took no further part in events in South Georgia or the Falklands.

9

Conclusion

In some of the foregoing chapters, difficulties with crews who thought redundancy was less desirable than volunteering to go to a war zone have highlighted the state of parts of the Merchant Navy in 1982. In the following years, the decline in the numbers of Merchant Navy personnel accelerated, and the logistics of moving large numbers of military personnel and their supporting stores and equipment has changed significantly.

So the question raised at the end of the Introduction is one that can now be given more consideration. That is: if there were to be another conflict in that region, or elsewhere equally remote from the UK, would the same response by the Merchant Navy now be possible?

Looking first at the period in the immediate aftermath of the war, Bob Mitchell, who described the Merchant Navy as 'an essential part of Britain's defence strategy' during a debate in the House Commons on 30 July 1982, went on to say, 'if necessary, money should be made available to ensure that we in this country have a strong Merchant Navy.' And the minister responsible replied that 'The Falklands operation has highlighted the interdependence between Royal and Merchant Navies', and that 'close and continuing liaison' would persist between the Ministry of Defence and the shipping industry.

In the light of the further severe decline of the Merchant Navy over the following 30 years, those words now sound rather futile. Even at the time, the Minister of Trade and Transport in Margaret Thatcher's government, Nicholas Ridley, when asked what the government proposed to do about the severe decline in British shipping, gave an abusive reply, saying that they would rather see it disappear than offer any subsidy.[1]

Four years later a Bow Group paper by Sir Edward du Cann, a Conservative Member of Parliament, argued for a restoration of the merchant fleet and added that it was in 'catastrophic decline'. He concluded:

Britain's merchant fleet should be our fourth arm of defence, but the shortage of ships is our Achilles heel ... In

---

[1] Quoted in R Woodman, *Fiddler's Green*. Stroud, 2010, 445.

> wartime problems would be inevitable in attempting to requisition British-owned ships registered abroad or ships on the register of British dependencies. Yet the Ministry of Defence relies on this to bolster numbers available. It is a mythical Armada ... In all probability a second Falklands campaign could not now mounted. [2]

In 1988 the Merchant Shipping Act of that year provided, amongst other powers, for the establishment of a Merchant Navy Reserve. This did not happen, and no reserve exists. The government also announced an agreement with the Bahamas for an 'open registry scheme' (otherwise known as a flag of convenience) to make it easier for UK-owned vessels on its register to be available in war or other times of national crisis. Whether this agreement is still in place is unknown, and how much it would depend on the good will of the ship owner is unclear. It could probably be included as part of the 'mythical Armada'.

Mounting such an operation again would depend on having the ships and the men to man them. In the 30 years since the Falklands War there have been, inevitably, a great many changes in transportation. The cruising industry has grown hugely, and there are many more cruise liners of increasingly extreme designs. Many would not wish to venture into areas such as the Southern Ocean, where they were not designed to operate, preferring more tranquil waters, but there are some that could. So it could be argued that the transport of personnel by sea is possible.

The carriage of large numbers of personnel by air is now a credible alternative, by chartered airliners as well as by service transport (the RAF are shortly to receive fourteen large-capacity transports) – provided, of course, that there are appropriately sized, and undamaged, airfields available. However, as was pointed out by a master in the RFA, even if troops arrived within hours by air, they would then have to wait the appropriate number of days or weeks for their supplies and

---

[2] Quoted in L Butcher, Shipping: UK policy. UK Parliament Briefing Paper SN/BT/595, 2010.

equipment to arrive by sea.

Those supplies and equipment would now, to a large extent, be carried in containers. The increase in container shipping and the demise of the conventional break bulk cargo ship has brought great change. One of the reasons that conventional cargo ships were of benefit in the Falklands was the lack of shoreside container facilities at the time (a container port has since been constructed). The dominance of container shipping has made shoreside facilities much more widespread. The range of size of the ships, from small 'feeder' ships bringing containers from small terminals to major ports, through those ships designed to be able to pass through the Panama and Suez canals, to the very largest and latest generation of ships, carrying up to 18,000 containers at a time, gives a choice of sizes which could be used.

As a result of the tonnage tax introduced by the Labour Government in 2000, there has been an increase in the number of ships now registered under the Red Ensign. In some eyes, this may be considered as making the Red Ensign a quasi flag of convenience, and many of the ships now British flagged are not British owned – which means that they may not have a legal duty to accept a wartime charter, although a moral duty could be thought to be likely, depending on the ethos and views of the ship owning company. Ships would also need to be logistically available – and some of BP's River class were not available for charter in 1982 for that very reason. Enough ships could be available, therefore, but given the likely short notice and the widespread nature of the fleet, logistical problems would increase. No clear conclusion is possible.

But what of the manning of the ships? In 1982 all foreign crews were taken off, some who wished to serve leaving under protest, to be replaced by British crews. (An exception was the Indian crew on the *Uganda*, which was a hospital ship and therefore subject to different rules.) Are there enough British seafarers to crew the number of ships that might become available?

The intransigent attitudes of the crews shown in the accounts of Don Jarvis and David Ede are evidence of a trend that led to a further reduction of British crews and the introduction of more foreign crews. Historically, the British Merchant Navy had employed various nationalities, including Indian and Chinese, examples of which are seen in the accounts of the *Uganda* and *Sir Lancelot*. The crews that now became commonplace were from Eastern Europe and the Far East. The second factor, other than the intransigent attitude of the crew, were the costs: Western European crews (not just British) had significantly higher pay than the crews who were replacing them.

The manning of British-flagged ships by British nationals was diluted still further in 1995 when the government announced that the posts of master, chief officer and chief engineer, which since 1919 had been restricted to British, Commonwealth or Irish citizens, were to be open to any nationality provided they held a United Kingdom Certificate of Competency or its equivalent. The only exceptions were certain categories of ship including cruise ships, product tankers and roll-on/roll-off ferries. The numbers in the British Merchant Navy continued to decline, unsurprisingly, as there was now no requirement for a British cargo ship to have any British crew, other than the bare minimum required under the tonnage tax introduced by John Prescott.

In 1980 there were 30,000 Merchant Navy ratings at sea. By 2005 there were 9000, mainly serving in the Royal Fleet Auxiliary or on ferries. The current number of British merchant seafarers, of all ranks, stands at a little over 14,000. New recruits are few and do not attract government help. A current programme to attract ratings into the Merchant Navy does not realistically expect more than 50 to enrol in any year. Instead of being a governmental responsibility, the training of cadets is left largely to Trinity House, a leading maritime charity. A much greater proportion of the total number is officers and engineers, rather than crew. Whether enough officers, engineers or crew could be found at short notice to take over the number of ships that might be chartered or requisitioned is very doubtful.

There is one other factor that must be taken into account, and that is the decline in size of the Royal Navy, which will potentially result in an even greater reliance on the Merchant

Navy, placing even greater demands on a diminished, and still diminishing, workforce and a potentially unreliable number of ships available.

So, in the unforeseen circumstance of another distant conflict needing the Merchant Navy to provide support, although the ships *may* be available, our ability to man them seems impossible.

Finally, the last question would be that of political will. Would any future government be prepared to take such action again?

Bibliography

Books

BP Shipping. *Operation Corporate: BP Shipping Limited's Involvement in the Falklands Islands Crisis*. BP, London, 1982.

Critchley M. *Falklands Task Force Portfolio, Parts 1 & 2*. Maritime Books, Liskeard, 1984.

Drought C. *NP 1840: the Loss of the Atlantic Conveyor*. Countyvise, Birkenhead, 2003.

Fletcher Roberts DG. *Conways and the Falklands: 1914 to 1982 and in Between by Some Who Were There*. Dunstable, 1983.

Freedman L. *The Official History of the Falklands Campaign*. 2 volumes. Routledge, London, 2005.

Hart Dyke D. *Four Weeks in May: the Loss of HMS Coventry*. Atlantic Books, London, 2007.

Lippiett J. *War and Peas: Intimate Letters from the Falklands War 1982*. Pistol Post, Bosham, 2007.

McManners H. *Forgotten Voices of the Falklands: the Real Story of the Falklands War*. Ebury Press, London, 2008.

Muxworthy JL. *Canberra: the Great White Whale Goes to War*. P&O, London, 1982.

Middlemiss NL. *The British Tankers*. Shield Publications, Newcastle-upon-Tyne, 2005.

P&O Shipping. *P&O in the Falklands: a Pictorial Record, 5 April – 25 September 1982*. P&O, London, 1982.

Puddefoot G. *No Sea Too Rough. The Royal Fleet Auxiliary in the Falklands War: the Untold Story*. Chatham, London, 2007.

Rentell P. *Master Mariner: a Life Under Way*. Seafarer Books, Rendlesham, 2009.

Rossiter M. *Sink the Belgrano*. Bantam, London, 2007.

Smith D, Johnson-Allen J. *Voices from the Bridge: Recollections of Members of the Honourable Company of Master Mariners*. Seafarer Books, Rendlesham, 2010.

Talbot-Booth EC. *Talbot-Booth's Merchant Ships, Volumes 1–3*. Marinart, London, 1979.

Thatcher C. *QE2: Forty Years Famous*. Simon & Schuster, London, 2007.

Villar R. *Merchant Ships at War: the Falklands Experience*. Conway Maritime, London, 1984.

Warwick RW. *QE2: the Cunard Line Flagship Queen Elizabeth 2*, 3rd edition. Norton, London, 1999.

Wilson RA. *RMS St Helena and the South Atlantic Islands*. Whittles, Dunbeath, 2006.

Winton J. *Signals from the Falklands: the Navy in the Falklands Conflict*. Leo Cooper, London, 1995.

Woodman R. *Fiddler's Green: the Great Squandering, 1921–2010. A History of the British Merchant Navy, Volume 5*. History Press, Stroud, 2010.

Documents

Butcher L. Shipping: UK policy. UK Parliament Briefing Paper, SN/BT/595. 2010.

Valovcin P. Logistics Lessons for the Operations Commander: the Falklands War. US Naval War College, Newport, RI, 1992.

Index

Page numbers in **bold** refer to illustrations. A number preceded by **P** refers to a photograph in the plate section (with pages numbered **P1** to **P8**). Vessels' names are in *italic*.

John Johnson-Allen

John Johnson-Allen went to sea in 1961 as a navigating apprentice with the BP Tanker Company, staying with them until 1969 and leaving as second mate. He subsequently qualified as a chartered surveyor, spent two years teaching seamanship and technical English to Iranian ex-soldiers in the Maritime Studies Department at Lowestoft College, and taught RYA evening classes for twenty-two years. Retiring from full-time employment in 2004, he read for a Masters degree in maritime history at the Greenwich Maritime Institute, part of Greenwich University, and graduated in 2009. He is Chairman of the Institute of Seamanship, a member of the Society for Nautical Research, a Fellow of the Royal Institute of Navigation and an Associate Member of the Honourable Company of Master Mariners. Having owned various boats, he now has a Drascombe Dabber, which he sails in a leisurely manner on the Norfolk Broads. With David Smith, he is the author of *Voices From the Bridge* (Seafarer Books, 2010).